Unsinkable

SONIA RICOTTI

Best-selling author, *The Law of Attraction Plain and Simple*

Unsinkable

HOW TO BOUNCE BACK QUICKLY WHEN LIFE KNOCKS YOU DOWN

New Page Books
A division of The Career Press, Inc.
Pompton Plains, N.J.

UNSINKABLE
EDITED AND TYPESET BY KARA KUMPEL
Cover design by Joseph Sherman/Dutton and Sherman
Printed in the U.S.A.

To order this title, please call toll-free 1-800-CAREER-1 (NJ and Canada: 201-848-0310) to order using VISA or MasterCard, or for further information on books from Career Press.

The Career Press, Inc.
220 West Parkway, Unit 12
Pompton Plains, NJ 07444
www.careerpress.com
www.newpagebooks.com

Library of Congress Cataloging-in-Publication Data
Ricotti, Sonia, 1965-
    Unsinkable : how to bounce back quickly when life knocks you down / by Sonia Ricotti ; foreword by James Redfield.
        p. cm.
    Includes index.
    ISBN 978-1-60163-176-3 -- ISBN 978-1-60163-650-8 (ebook)
    1. Self-realization. 2. Love. 3. New Thought. I. Title.

BF637.S4R5723 2011
158.1--dc22

                                                        2011003528

I dedicate this book to you, the reader. May the message and lessons within these pages help you bounce back higher than you ever thought possible. Great things are waiting for you around the corner.

This book is also dedicated to my brother, Tony Ricotti. Without his support and love, this book and the work I do would never have been possible.

To my extraordinary and loving parents, Marlene and Roberto Ricotti: I love you.

Acknowledgments

First and foremost, I must say thank you to my brother, Tony Ricotti, for always being there for me when I needed him most, for picking me up when I was knocked down, and for being my saving grace. Words cannot express the gratitude and love I feel for you. You are not just a brother to me; you are my best friend; you are my angel.

I also thank:

My parents, Marlene and Roberto, for demonstrating what true unconditional love is all about throughout the years. I love you, Mom and Dad.

Bill Gladstone, my literary agent. Fate brought us together. My angels were looking out for me that day. Thank you for believing in this message and this book.

Danielle Joffe, for being such a great and true friend for so many years and for always being there for me.

Melinda Asztalos—"Wow" is all I can say. You have incredible strength and a positive outlook on life, and your inner light is always shining. Thank you for allowing me into your life while going through your most challenging and vulnerable moments, and also for sharing your story. You have been my teacher.

Cindy Ashton, for helping me during my challenging times and for being there whenever I needed you.

Bob Doyle, for being such a great friend and always being willing to help when I need a hand. Your sense of humor always puts a smile on my face.

Dr. Brett Moore, my chiropractor for many years, for always being available to adjust me on such short notice and for supporting my work. Helping me keep my "power on" has helped tremendously with the writing of this book.

Sam Cawthorn, my new friend from Down Under. I am so happy you're alive! Thank you for being such a positive, bright light on this planet, and for contributing your incredible story to this book.

Gina Mollicone-Long, for helping me out when I needed it, for being a great friend, and for contributing your words of wisdom to this book.

James Redfield, for writing the Foreword to this book and for being such an incredible pure bright light on this earth.

Cynthia Kersey, for sharing your powerful message to this book and for making a difference in so many people's lives around the globe. You are a true inspiration.

Marci Shimoff, for sharing your message of unconditional love to this book and for being a true living example of what you teach—your message of love is something the world desperately needs today.

Bob Proctor, for sharing your very personal story and lending your unsinkable words of wisdom to this book. You are an inspiration to people around the world.

Joann Brnjas, for sharing your beautiful message of hope with the world. Samantha will live in our hearts forever.

Janet Attwood, for being the amazing and loving person that you are and for sharing your inspirational story to this book.

My friends at New Page Books, for believing in me and my Unsinkable message and for your professionalism and patience throughout the publishing process of this book.

Melina Zeppieri, for being one of my biggest supporters, for always being there whenever I need you, and for being the beautiful loving person that you are.

Contents

Foreword by James Redfield   15

Preface   19

Introduction   23

Chapter 1: First Things First   41

#1: Say Yes! *to Change*

#2: It's Okay to Feel Bad

#3: You Are Not Alone

#4: Create a Circle of Light

#5: Learn or Recycle

Chapter 2: Surrender, Let Go, and Have Faith   61

#6: Surrender to What Is

#7: Let Go of What Was

#8: Have Faith in What Will Be

Chapter 3: Master Your Mind   91

#9: Re-Create Your Reality

#10: Shed Your Limiting Beliefs

#11: Step Away From the Closed Door

Chapter 4: Connect to Your Higher Self   115

#12: Be Good to Yourself

#13: Listen to the Whispers

#14: Just "Be"

Chapter 5: Let Love Lead   131

#15: Forgive Yourself and Others

#16: Always Come From a Place of Love

#17: Be Grateful for All That Is and All That Will Be

Chapter 6: Give to Feel Good   153

#18: Step Outside of Yourself

Chapter 7: Step Into Your Greatness   161

#19: Within Every Crisis Lies a Golden Opportunity

#20: Live a Maverick Life

Conclusion: Rising From the Ashes   171

Epilogue   177

Resources   179

Appendix: Biographies of Unsinkable Contributors   181

Index   187

About the Author   191

Foreword
by James Redfield

Do you feel it? There's something happening out there. Some say it's a new level of authenticity. The Mayan calendar suggests it's a new wave of consciousness entering all of humanity, just when we need it the most. I would call it an emerging Twelfth Insight, where we're learning to live our innermost spiritual knowledge.

But regardless of what we call it, we feel as though a greater part of ourselves is coming in to strengthen and enlarge our souls. And it seems, well, natural, as though we're discovering some greater Divine reconnection that feels like coming home.

One of the changes born of this new consciousness is learning how to handle the personal crises of life. Far from foolishly seeking to avoid all trouble, or trying to insulate ourselves so completely that we never have to feel pain, this new approach helps us in a better way: It leads us to a place where—believe it or not—we can find a higher purpose in the heartache, as though it was an experience that was necessary if we are to become the person we were meant to be.

This higher journey through the experience of crisis is the subject of this wonderful book. Sonia Ricotti has been through the storms herself and now sees the process through the longer lens of spiritual growth. I would even say this is a Twelfth Insight book, because it assumes that each of us can discover an inner strategy that can handle all the challenges that come our way—so much so that we become unsinkable.

For starters, Sonia takes us through a centering process that moves us into what will be the greatest discovery of our age: the ability to surrender to a higher God Connection and Guidance. The God Connection is key, because it brings us the peace and love that in troubled times restores our bearings. After that, the Intuitive Guidance kicks in, and we realize that we're in a particular situation for a higher purpose: to break through some bad habit, or to stretch into a new understanding of ourselves and of life. Mostly the experience reveals a certain talent we have through which we can touch and help others. Always it is about becoming a new, more conscious person.

Experts say our personal crises tend to happen at certain times in life. First there are the courtship heartbreaks that tend to occur in the teens and 20s. At age 30 or so, there are the problems of finding worldly success in our careers. In our 40s comes the usual crisis of the soul: Am I doing what I was really meant to do with my life? Of course, illness, breakups, or losing a loved one can happen anytime. All can rock our world and leave us emotionally paralyzed for a time.

Perhaps this foreword is even sounding a bit too cerebral to you right now. That's okay. Do as Sonia suggests: Don't think too much at first, just have faith and trust until you see the light at the end of the tunnel. It's there, and this book can guide you through the twists and turns that lead you to it.

Preface

I don't know from where I got the title "Unsinkable." It seems as though one day I just started using the term in my everyday life. I know it entered my vocabulary toward the end of my difficult journey, as I was reaching the end of the tunnel and beginning to see the light.

I recently looked up the word *unsinkable* and found this World English Dictionary definition:

Unsinkable: Not capable of sinking or being sunk.

The word seemed such a perfect metaphor for when we are going through challenging times and doing our best to survive and get through it (and not sink). We are trying to stay afloat.

This book came about because of the trials and tribulations I experienced in my life. There were times when I felt I was drowning, when I was trying so hard to swim against the current and was left feeling that I just couldn't do it anymore. Other times, I would simply float and surrender to the current. One journey was difficult and tiring; the other was peaceful and calming.

Through time, I have been blessed with meeting some incredible people who have experienced some seemingly insurmountable life challenges, yet managed to get through them unscathed, and ended up even happier than they'd been before. I had to study them. I needed to learn from them. What was the secret to being peaceful and happy even in the face of despair? How do you bounce back quickly when life knocks you down?

I will be sharing their dramatic and inspirational stories and the lessons I learned from them.

I also interviewed many high-profile self-help authors and professionals through a teleseminar series I hosted called "Be Unsinkable." I was amazed to discover a common theme among each and every one of them, though each had his or her own way of sharing and teaching the message. Some of them have contributed their unsinkable words of wisdom to this book as well.

This book is not one you read and cast aside; it is a book you will refer to over and over again. It is a journey. It is a book you integrate into your everyday life from this day forward. You see, it isn't about just getting through *this* difficult situation or time; it is about gliding through *all* situations that are thrown your way, in the future as well.

The tools, tips, stories, and steps in this book will transform your experience of life itself. You may not be able to control your circumstances at the moment, but what you can control is your reaction to them and how you choose to experience them. This book will guide you to that ultimate state of mind where you are happy no matter what life throws at you. Sure, you'll still have those moments of anger, frustration, and sadness, but they will be short-lived. You will experience those emotions and then move forward in peace and with power.

You see, this book isn't just about bouncing back quickly when life knocks you down; it is about bouncing back higher than you ever thought possible. It is about achieving greatness not *despite* what has happened in your life, but *because* of what has happened in your life.

I have experienced my own share of let-downs and massive change in my life throughout the years, and had those "negative" experiences not happened to me, I wouldn't be sharing this book and this important message with you today.

See? Everything happens for a reason.

Introduction

As we stood in the driveway between our two parked cars, ready to say our final goodbyes, I was an empty shell, numb on the inside. Part of me was still desperately holding on to the past, and the other part of me was being reluctantly pushed into the unknown future.

Both our cars were packed to the rim with boxes, the last items left in the house. The moving truck had already taken all the big items. Our big beautiful home was empty now. As empty as my heart was feeling at that moment.

It was time to say goodbye. This was it. The end of a life I knew so well. The end.

Of course with every end, there is a new beginning. I just didn't know what this new beginning was going to look like yet. I did know what the end looked like though, and the searing pain in my heart of saying goodbye to "what was" was unbearable.

The piercing pain of this tremendous loss felt like I had been stabbed repeatedly in my heart.

I was saying goodbye to the man I loved with all my heart. He was my soulmate, my best friend, and my biggest supporter in life and my career. I was saying goodbye to my amazing step-kids, whom I knew after this day I would only see on occasion. I was saying goodbye to the house I called home. And I was saying goodbye to a life that at one time was so perfect.

Yes, perfect. At one time, it was all perfect.

A Year to Remember

The year prior to that moment was quite the roller-coaster ride. In fact, it was the most difficult and challenging year of my life. As I think back to all the events that occurred, I realize I could probably write *several* books just on my story: one on dealing with serious health issues (a dangerous blood clot); one on dealing with financial devastation and losing everything (including my home); one on living with an alcoholic partner (that alone can be a *series* of books); one on dealing with a relationship breakup; and a final one on starting over.

Although my experience had left me feeling raw, exposed, and vulnerable, the lessons I learned and the growth I experienced are what helped me reinvent myself and reach the proverbial mountaintop.

As I look back now at what happened, I realize that everything happened exactly the way it was supposed to.

Today, after the storm has passed and the sun is shining again (brighter than ever!), I realize it was something that needed to happen in order for me to blossom into the person I am today. I am grateful for it all. It was a gift.

I can't believe this is all happening to me. One thing I know for sure: Something great is going to come out of this. I don't know what yet, but something amazing, huge, and incredible will come out of it. Something so big; way bigger than me. I will make sure of it, because there is no way I am going through all this for nothing!

Those were the words I said to myself when I hit rock bottom.

I remember exactly where I was (in my bedroom) and where I was standing (at the window looking outside). I had just had a major meltdown. My face was still streaked with salty tears. My eyes were bloodshot and swollen from crying. I felt defeated, lost, and helpless. I didn't know which way to turn, what to do, or how I was going to get out of my situation.

Yet, I had faith. I believed.

I have no idea where this strength came from. In fact, just moments before, I had wanted to end it all. The pain was so unbearable. My heart felt like it was being ripped apart. I just wanted the pain to stop.

Moments earlier

"Why is this happening? Why?! Why?!"

Those were the only words I could muster through my sobs of desperation. The pain I felt inside me was unbearable. I had never felt such a deep pain.

"I don't know," my life partner whispered quietly in my ear. "I don't know."

He held me close as we lay there together on the bed in a spooning position. I was curled up like a ball, like a child. We lay there quietly for what seemed like an eternity. I was at the end of my rope. I just couldn't do it anymore. Life had become too hard and painful to go on. Everything in my life seemed to be slipping away. I felt like I was drowning.

The thought of ending it all seemed like the only way to end this pain. I thought about it for a moment. Then, I began to sob more and louder than before. I realized that ending it all just wasn't even an option. If I were to do that, the people in my life who love me would be devastated, and the thought of all the pain my demise would cause made me even more depressed and desperate. I knew that my mother and father would never recover from such a tragedy (losing their one and only daughter), and my brother, who was my best friend, would never be the same again. The thought of bringing deep sadness and pain to their lives (like the pain I was feeling at that moment) was something I did not want to do.

Wow, I thought to myself, *I really* don't *have any options!*

I continued to sob uncontrollably.

What Was

What is amazing is that, a while back, I was basking in the spotlight of being a #1 best-selling author of my very first book. I was busy doing TV interviews, radio interviews, book signings, and speaking events. My business, Lead Out Loud, was morphing into something absolutely amazing, offering inspiration, hope, and help to people everywhere around the world. I was healthy and fit as a fiddle. I had found the love of my life (finally!) and was an instant step-mom to his two amazing children. I was on top of the world!

Everything was picture perfect.

When Life Takes an Unexpected Turn

How does one go from living a happy, successful life filled with love, harmony, and abundance, to thinking that ending it all might be the only soothing option?

I wondered how all this happened in the first place. I wondered how I "attracted" all of this into my life. For those of you who don't know me, I wrote a best-seller titled *The Law of Attraction Plain and Simple*. In this book, I explained an 11-step process of how to manifest the life of your dreams. In fact, the book was hailed as taking the blockbuster hit and DVD *The Secret* to the next level. I explain in the book what the Law of Attraction is and how to master being a deliberate manifestor to achieve everything and anything you want in life.

If you are not familiar with concept of The Law of Attraction, I describe it in the book this way: The Law of Attraction is a universal law that is present at all times. Put simply, it means that like attracts like. The Law of Attraction states that thought energy and projected energy attract similar energy. Simply stated, we attract into our lives whatever we direct our conscious attention to.

Because I know how the Law of Attraction works, I wondered how I attracted this mess into my life. How did I go from masterfully attracting the life of my dreams to actually losing it all? At first, I was scratching my head wondering where I went wrong. The truth is, I *didn't* go wrong; everything happened *exactly* the way it was supposed to.

You see, one of my goals all along was to make a difference in the world. I wanted to be able to share my inspirational message to thousands of people at a time at large venues around the globe. Each day, I visualized myself speaking on a stage to thousands and tens of thousands of people at a time.

I had no idea how that would manifest in my life, but of course, I had all the tools and knowledge I needed to make it happen. What I didn't realize was that in order for me to achieve that goal and dream I would need to let go and leave behind the life I had been desperately holding on to.

It was all unfolding with exact precision.

As I look back now, I can see precisely when the first signs of the difficult times ahead appeared. Of course, at the time, I was completely oblivious to them. Or perhaps I chose to ignore them. Things were just too perfect to pay attention to the red flags.

One day, I had just returned home from shopping as the phone rang. I put my bags down and ran to answer it. I already knew who it was.

"Hi hun! You just caught me in time. I just got in the door." I said.

"Oh great. Where were you?" he asked.

"I just picked up a few items from Wal-Mart."

"Wal-Mart?"

"Yeah, Wal-Mart."

"How can you shop at Wal-Mart? I can't believe you would shop there!" he said in an accusatory tone.

We had been dating for a couple of months, and we were so happy to have found each other. We had both been looking for our soulmate, and thought the search was finally over.

"Why are you saying that?" I asked, wondering where he was going with this.

"You shouldn't shop there." he said. "Wal-Mart is the enemy to small businesses! They have monopolized the market, and thousands and thousands of small businesses have closed down because of them." He was becoming very agitated. "They're also ripping off all their suppliers by paying very low prices for the merchandise. No one should shop at Wal-Mart!"

I was taken aback by his comments and his aggressive tone. He was really adamant that no one should shop at Wal-Mart, and I was feeling judged for shopping there. Feeling a little annoyed, I replied defensively, "Well, I *like* shopping there. Their prices are low and they have a huge selection of everything. You can have your own opinion on it, but I'm going to continue shopping there."

For the next 30 minutes or so, he went on and on about how *Wal-Mart is the enemy* and *no one should shop there.* Eventually, I started tuning him out. The whole conversation was bizarre. He was really upset and felt very strongly about the topic. I had never seen that side of him. I thought to myself, *Wow, he really doesn't like Wal-Mart!*

The next day, he called me again. This time I was lounging around at home. As we were talking on the phone, I could hear him eating something.

"Hey, what are you eating?" I asked.

"Chocolate-covered licorice."

The thought of eating chocolate-covered licorice made me sick to my stomach. "Chocolate-covered licorice? Where did you get *that*?" I asked. His reply floored me.

"Wal-Mart."

I realized that something was really off here. I didn't know *what* exactly, but it was really bizarre. We never spoke of that "Wal-Mart" conversation ever again. I chose to ignore the red flag. In fact, we even shopped together at Wal-Mart many, many times after that phone discussion.

I later realized (much later) that he was drinking the evening the Wal-Mart rant took place. He was an alcoholic. He was what they call a "functioning" alcoholic. It was something that was hidden from me for a long time. Alcoholism was new to me. I had never been exposed to that world before. In fact, I didn't even drink, at all. I was soon to become very well acquainted with that world.

Many months would go by before I realized he had a problem. I had moved into his big, beautiful home, and he asked me to marry him. We traveled the world together. I became very close to his two amazing children, and I quickly took on the role of step-parent with great enjoyment.

The recession hit us hard in 2008. Many months went by and the economy was just not picking up. Although *my* business was thriving, it wasn't enough to keep both of us afloat. The threat of losing everything (including the home we lived in) was becoming quickly apparent. The financial strain on his business, along with the reality that he may lose it all, had taken him over the edge, and his drinking became a very obvious and serious problem.

Every once in a while there would be a glimmer of hope. For instance, he knew he had a drinking problem, and on a few occasions he would attend Alcoholics Anonymous meetings. When he did, I would wish and pray that *this time* he would finally beat this addiction. Each time he would remain sober for a short while, but he would eventually go back to drinking. It was an endless, heartbreaking cycle. As much as I wanted to help him, I knew that his addiction was completely out of my control. This was difficult for me to accept. I wished with every fiber of my being that I could help him. I also knew that if something didn't change, our relationship would not last. He knew this too.

To make matters worse, I woke up one morning with a mild, throbbing pain under my left arm. I thought I had somehow pulled a muscle, and ignored it. A few days later, the pain intensified, so I had it checked out. I'll never forget the doctor's words: "Well, Sonia, I have the results. I'm afraid it isn't good news. I'm sure this isn't what you were expecting to hear. You have a blood clot. A very dangerous blood clot. The location of the blood clot under your left arm is a cause for serious concern. The clot's current location is very close to your lungs and heart; if it dislodges, it can be fatal. You need immediate emergency treatment."

My initial reaction was denial. *This just can't be*, I thought. *I feel fine. I've never felt better. There is no way this is a possibly fatal blood clot. No way. They made a mistake.* I even argued with the doctor about it. I asked him to go and double check and make sure that there wasn't a mistake. He left the room to go "double-check" the results. Ten minutes later he returned and confirmed the diagnosis. Possible fatal blood clot it is.

The doctor continued to ask me questions. He said that this was a very odd location to have a blood clot, and wondered if I had been in a car accident or if someone had hit me. I said no to both questions. He said he wanted to do several tests to find out the reason why this blood clot developed. Next thing I know, I was quickly sent down the hallway to have bloodwork done for further testing. They took 11 vials of blood. I was then brought to the Thrombosis Clinic section of the hospital where I met with a nurse who was going to begin administering my treatment. I wasn't sure what to expect, and I didn't quite understand what was going on at that point.

She began to explain how the treatment was going to be administered and how it will all work. "In the past, someone with your condition would require immediate hospitalization to get treatment," she said very calmly.

Great! No hospitalization! I thought to myself.

"Today, we are able to treat patients by having them administer the treatment themselves. The medication is called Heparin and you simply inject the medication daily into your abdomen area." She said nonchalantly. *What? She expects me to self-inject this medication into my abdomen? Is she insane?*

"Oh, no. That's never going to happen. I'm sorry. I am petrified of needles. I can't even look at a needle without feeling nauseous. I'm sorry, that is not an option." I said with a tinge of panic in my voice. "Can't you just give me some pills instead?"

"No. This treatment must be administered this way. The other option is to come to the hospital every day and have a nurse inject it for you," she replied. *Come to the hospital every day? The hospital is a 35 minute drive away; that would be really inconvenient,* I thought to myself.

"Why don't I give you your first injection right now and show you how it's done. Then you can decide if you want to do it yourself or whether you want to return to the hospital every day," she said. "Don't worry, it won't hurt a bit"

"Okay," I said hesitantly.

She took the needle out. It was the biggest needle I had ever seen. She proceeded to demonstrate to me how to get the thick yellow liquid out of the bottle with the needle, pointed out the area where to inject it, explained how to inject it, and so on. She injected the serum into my abdomen very slowly.

"See, it's no big deal. You may feel a little pain or a slight burning sensation but it will go away," she said. *Slight burning? Are you kidding me? Hey lady, have you ever been injected with this stuff before? My stomach is on fire!* is what I was thinking. *Be brave. Be brave. Stop being such a big baby.*

"Oh yeah, I guess it's not so bad," I said.

I decided to try injecting myself at home each day and see how it goes. As I was driving home with my big stash of needles and vials of medication on my passenger seat, a bizarre thought entered my mind. What if that blood clot dislodges right now and travels to my heart and lungs, and I die?

All of a sudden all the things in my life that seemed so urgent and important no longer seemed important at all anymore. In fact, it all seemed so trivial. For instance, at the time, I was in the process of organizing a major product launch and we were very behind schedule. But at that moment, I couldn't have cared less. Nothing work-related or money-related was important at that moment. All that mattered were the amazing people in my life. It sounds very cliché, I know, but it is true. A sense of peace came over my body and mind. It was okay to let go of the stress I had been holding on to from all the trivial stuff in my life. At that moment I realized it was *all* trivial.

Never in a million years would I ever have imagined being able to inject myself with a needle, yet somehow I managed to do it every day for 21 days straight until my next appointment with the doctor at the Thrombosis Clinic. I can't say I was good at it though. My entire abdominal area was one big bruise.

It was then time to meet with my doctor to discuss the results of the bloodwork and decide what further treatment to begin. He opened my file that had all the test results and began shaking his head.

"I don't understand this," he said. "Everything came back negative. We were hoping to find out through these tests why you developed this blood clot, but everything came back normal. This is really bizarre. Are you sure no one hit you?"

"No one hit me, I can assure you. I would remember if someone hit me."

"Because we are unable to determine why you developed this blood clot and your results came back insignificant, what I think I will do is simply take you off all medication. No further treatment for now," he said. "However, please have a very low tolerance for any symptoms. If you begin experiencing symptoms again, don't wait; come straight to the hospital."

I wasn't sure if I should be happy or worried at that moment. I was happy that I didn't have to inject myself with needles anymore, but worried about the possibility of another clot developing. For the next several months I was on heightened alert for any possible symptoms.

With so many negative events happening at one time, I felt as though everything was spiraling out of control. The next few months were a test. Many lessons would be learned (which I share in this book), immense growth would take place, and the meaning of letting go, accepting what is, and offering unconditional love would take on a whole new meaning.

Little did I know that my purpose on this earth was about to shift, that an awakening was about to take place, and that a new book was about to be written.

Finding Peace in the Midst of Chaos

As I walked (and stumbled) upon my life path through the next few months, I realized I was lucky. I was lucky because I had already begun my path of self-discovery. I knew what was required to get through these tough times with grace and ease, and how to find inner peace and joy even in the midst of chaos. In fact, I had been teaching these concepts in all my workshops, created audio programs, and talked about them on my radio show.

What I didn't realize was how difficult it would be.

I am not going to lie to you and say it is going to be easy, because it isn't. I'm not going to say that by simply reading this book, you will find peace and everything is going to be okay. I'm not going to say that when you wake up tomorrow morning, everything is going to be picture perfect, because, chances are, it isn't (although you never know!).

What I am saying is that life is a journey, and although you will be faced with challenges along the way (many of which will be circumstances out of your control), you have the ability to choose how you deal with them, how you interpret them, and how you react to them. Although you may feel that you don't have much of a choice, it isn't so. You *do* have a choice.

You have the choice of gliding through it with peace and joy or suffering through it with anger, frustration, and resentment.

Anyone in their right mind would choose peace and joy instead of suffering. So why doesn't everyone choose this obviously better path? Because many people aren't even aware that this choice even exists. Awareness is key.

You have direct access to inner peace and joy at any given moment. It isn't something you search for, something you buy, or something someone else gives you. It is within you. In fact, you have access to it right now. Right this second.

You hold the key to this beautiful place of serenity and bliss. Access to this world is not determined by what is occurring in the external world. In fact, everything can be changing in your life and negative events can be unfolding in the world outside of you, but that doesn't matter. What does matter is what choices you make in your *inner* world.

You can be confronted with challenging circumstances that make it seem as though everything is falling apart all around you, and still experience true inner peace and joy. You can also have everything going well in your life and yet be unhappy, stressed, and have your mind filled with chaos and dissatisfaction.

The sooner you realize that what is going on around you is irrelevant to your true joy and peace, and that you have immediate access to this beautiful world, the sooner you can begin loving life—no matter what happens.

This doesn't happen overnight, of course; it takes some commitment and dedication to achieve this ultimate state of mind. It isn't always easy to gain access to this beautiful "place" either, but with practice, it gets easier and easier. It's there. Always know it's there.

In the next section of this book, I will be sharing with you 20 life lessons. These lessons are filled with insight, relatable stories, and tips that will help you get through your current difficult situation with grace and ease; it will help you bounce back quickly, and higher than you ever thought possible. You will have direct access to peace and joy whenever you choose.

Be patient; it is a process. Have faith; it will happen. It happened to me.

20 Powerful Lessons to Live by When Life Knocks You Down

Chapter 1:
First Things First

When you come to the end of your rope, tie a knot and hang on.
—Franklin D. Roosevelt

#1: Say *Yes!* to Change

You've probably heard the old quote from Benjamin Franklin: "The only things certain in life are death and taxes." As funny (and true) as that statement is, I'd like to add one more thing to it: change. Change is definitely "certain in life."

Change is inevitable. It is happening all the time. As much as we'd love to hold on to the safety and comfort of the known, we all come to a place in our lives where we are required to take the road of uncertainty.

Of course, you have a choice of how you experience that path. You can choose to be dragged down that path kicking and screaming, or you can say yes to change and embrace it! When you say yes to change, you are choosing to navigate that path peacefully and happily, and see where it takes you.

It doesn't matter which way you choose to take that path; change is going to happen anyway. The peaceful and happy path is the ideal way to experience change. It is also the best way to reach your new destination in record time.

This is a distressing time for you, no doubt, and how you choose to react to this situation will determine your outcome. It will determine how quickly you bounce back from the experience, and whether you bounce back higher.

Of course, when you say no to change and you are dragged down that path with anger, frustration, and sadness, your journey and recovery will be a long and difficult one (some people never fully recover). When you say yes to change and surrender to what is happening, your journey will be more pleasant and peaceful, and the recovery time will be shorter.

Whenever you are in a situation in which your life has taken an unexpected turn, embrace it. You may not know what the future holds, and fear of the unknown can sometimes be overwhelming and nerve-wracking, but just remember you have a choice of how to react to this situation. Choose the path of least resistance.

It is all happening for a reason, and although you may not be clear on what the reason is right now or what the future holds exactly, have faith that things will turn out beautifully.

You may remember Bob Proctor from the blockbuster hit DVD and book *The Secret*. He is one of the most respected experts in the self-help world. Bob recently experienced a serious challenge in his own life, and I wondered how he (of all people) handled life's difficult challenges and what he did to overcome his obstacles and bounce back quickly. This is his story, and his unsinkable words of wisdom.

BOB PROCTOR'S MESSAGE

I remember it was a Saturday. I was listening to Michael Beckwith speak at a conference. He shared a three-step approach to use whenever anything happens in your life.

1. It is what it is; accept it. (It's either going to control you or you're going to control it.)

2. Harvest the good.

3. Forgive all the rest.

Sunday, it was my turn to speak, and after I finished my talk, I wasn't feeling well. A doctor who had been at the conference had a clinic five minutes from the hotel where I was staying. He came to see me, gave me a B-12 shot, and said that I should feel better. The next day, Monday, he told me to come to his clinic to get some bloodwork done, and wanted to know when I was returning to Toronto. I told him I was flying back on Thursday, so he advised me to return to see him on Wednesday to get the results of the bloodwork. I returned on Wednesday as requested, and while he was checking me over, he held a stethoscope to my heart and said, "You can't get on a plane tomorrow. You have a problem here."

The following week I was in the hospital having open-heart surgery. They replaced the aortic valve; in order to do this, they had to stop my heart, collapse my lungs, and put me on a machine to keep me alive. It was a radical operation. When I came out of it all I could remember were Michael Beckwith's words: *It is what it is; accept it. (It's either going to control you or you're going to control it.) Harvest the good. Forgive all the rest.*

I had the best care in the world. I got to know the name of every nurse and every doctor that came into my room. I told the doctor, "This has to be the best hospital in the world; everyone has such a great attitude." He said, "Well, they like looking after you because *you* have such a great attitude. You call them all by name and treat them well." I told him about Michael Beckwith's advice that I was following. I have since shared it with hundreds of thousands of people, and have incorporated it into every area of my life. Those three statements will help you through any situation.

I was told that I would be laid up for six months, but I was back on the road in three. I've been fine ever since.

Stop and Think

When you find yourself in a difficult situation, you need to stop and think. Remember, it will control you or you will control it, so take control. Harvest the good (look for the good in the situation), and forgive all the rest. Let the rest go.

Victor Frankl said, "It's the last of all human freedoms, the ability to choose." We can choose to look at whatever we want. We can look at what's wrong in our life or we can look at what's right.

Sometimes tragedy will just grab ahold of our mind and won't let go. We have to let it go. We have to look for the good; there's good in everything. The more you look, the more you will find. We're only going to see what we're in resonance or in harmony with, so if we're thinking good thoughts and sending out good energy, then we start to see all kinds of good things, and they begin to compound.

Look for the good and forgive all the rest. If a bad thought arises, just forgive it and let it go. Of course, bad thoughts will come. You may pick them up from outside sources or they may originate from you, but when they do arise, don't spend any time on them or give any room in your mind to them. Just release them.

Send Love and Let it Go

Having bad thoughts such as hate, anger, or resentment toward another person is comparable to *you* drinking rat poison and hoping *the rats* die. What we need is understanding. We have to understand that there's a beautiful power flowing in our consciousness, and as that power flows in, it has no form. *We* give it form. So if we choose to hold bad thoughts about someone, we must realize that we will move into a bad vibration and will attract more bad things into our lives. Instead, learn how to let these thoughts go. Simply release them and send love to the people who bother you.

Here is something you can do to help you to release negative thoughts and feelings.

1. Each morning when you wake up, sit down and think of 10 things you are grateful for and really allow yourself to feel the emotions come through.

2. Then, be still and relax for four or five minutes and ask for guidance for the day. The answers will come.

3. Send love to the people who bother you.

This early morning practice may be difficult at first, but with time you will master it.

Help Others

I believe that when we're having problems, no matter what kind they may be, our focus is on ourselves. It's all about me, me, me; we become very self-conscious and self-indulgent. When this happens, it is important to train ourselves to think about others instead. We have to get our mind off of ourselves. Simply think of other people, and focus on how to help them and how to provide greater service to them. When we do this, we move into a good vibration and thus will attract good into our lives.

You Really *Are* in Control

Pogo said, "We have met the enemy and he is us." I believe this. We cause our own problems. It has been 50 years since I picked up and studied Napoleon Hill's book *Think and Grow Rich*. The man who gave me that book would say, "You're the only problem you'll ever have and you're the only solution." I think it took me five years to understand what he meant by that. There's a lot of wisdom in those words. No one else can ever cause us a problem without our permission.

So we really *are* in control.

Dr. J.B. Rhine said, "The mind is the greatest power in all of creation." When I say this in seminars, I often hear some people say, "No, *God* is the greatest." I say, God is the *creator*, the mind is a creation, and you have access to this marvelous mind. What we have to learn to do is utilize it properly.

Ultimately, I believe that when something tragic happens to us, it has been sent to us to strengthen us. I know I'm a much better person today. I'm much more empathetic with people in seminars who have problems. My experience has truly strengthened me.

#2: It's Okay to Feel Bad

Let the tears flow; it's okay. In fact, it is necessary to your healing.

That day when I left the house and everything behind me, I remember calling my friend Cindy Ashton. She was no stranger to life challenges. In fact, she underwent three heart surgeries by the age of 14 and was left in chronic pain, with a damaged lung. Today, she is a brilliant performer, singer, and motivational speaker.

She asked me, "So how are you feeling?"

I replied, "I'm okay. I'm surprised how well I'm handling this."

"You know it's okay to cry," she said. "You need to let it all out and release it."

"Yeah, I know. But I don't feel like crying. It's weird."

It *was* weird. *Why am I not crying? Could this be it? Am I ready to put everything behind me and move forward already? Wow, I must be superwoman!*

"Well, you'll release it when you're ready. Don't resist it though," she said.

"You know, I can't cry. I don't know why, I just can't," I said.

"Well, I'm sure it will come. When it does, just let the tears flow."

I thought to myself, *I'm okay. I'll be fine. I don't need or feel like crying. I'm done. I'm ready to move forward.*

Two hours later I was curled up like a ball on my bed, bawling my eyes out like a child. I was crying an uncontrollable river of tears. The pain was more fierce than any I had ever experienced. It lingered, along with the tears, for many, many hours. A deluge of emotions came over me. I was angry. I was sad. I was resentful. I was playing the victim so beautifully well, asking, *Why me?!* I don't remember ever crying as much or for as long as I did that day.

What I do remember is that when I finally got myself out of bed (with my bloodshot and swollen eyes), I felt better. I remember consciously giving myself permission to feel what I was feeling without judging it. I allowed myself to feel angry, sad, and resentful, and play the victim. In fact, I welcomed it.

Throughout the years, we have been conditioned to believe that crying is a negative thing. "Stop crying!" is what I hear parents tell their children all the time. We have been conditioned to keep our "negative" feelings to ourselves; in reality, it is the worst thing we can do. By keeping our sadness and pain on the inside, we are not making it go away. Instead, we are holding on to it. In essence, we are prolonging the agonizing journey. Some people keep themselves "busy" in order to forget their problems and avoid dealing with feeling what they are feeling. This avoidance, too, will prolong the distressing journey.

The purging of negative emotions that are bottled up inside you is cathartic and therapeutic, and, once released, allows a space and opening for clarity, peace, and the ability to move forward.

A Common Misconception About the Law of Attraction

Some people who are firm believers in the Law of Attraction think that feeling and expressing negative emotions will generate negative energy, and therefore attract negative things, people, and situations into their lives. Yes, it is true that like energy attracts like energy, but I have one question for you: Which do you think is worse, generating negative energy for a few hours and releasing it, or unconsciously holding on to it and carrying it with you for years and years?

You see, by not releasing your pain and sadness and avoiding your feelings, you are unconsciously generating negative energy. Suppressing your negative feelings may feel better in the short run, but it will have devastating effects on your life in the long run. In fact, when you don't deal with those feelings, you are walking around with this negativity with you all the time. Imagine yourself walking around with an invisible anchor attached to your leg, dragging it around with you everywhere you go. You can't see it, but it is making moving forward in your life really difficult and uncomfortable.

The sooner you release your feelings, the quicker you will get to the other side, and the sooner you will bounce back higher than you ever thought possible.

> ## Tip
>
> A great way to unleash your true feelings is to write them out. Buy a journal and write in it each day. Journaling is a powerful and therapeutic activity. It is like having a conversation with yourself.
>
> When writing, don't think about what you are writing; just write whatever comes to your mind. Don't edit it, question it, or judge it. Simply write freely, as though the words are being channeled through you. Allow whatever comes up to come up. If you feel like crying, allow yourself to cry. Allow yourself to feel the pain. Allow all the pain, sadness, and anger to come to the surface, and release it. Don't think it is wrong to feel what you are feeling.
>
> Sometimes nothing feels better than a good cry.

#3: You Are Not Alone

Sometimes when we are going through a crisis, we feel very alone. We get so deep into our own story and situation that we forget that there is a world outside of us.

I remember during a radio interview I gave a while ago, I had just finished recounting my story and sharing everything that happened to me when a caller's comment really struck me: "Please don't take this the wrong way, but boy am I happy to hear your story and know that someone else is going through this kind of stuff! It feels good to know that I am not the only one."

I laughed. It's true. It is easy to fall into the "poor me" trap and feel completely isolated and alone. In fact, it may seem as though everyone's lives all around you are so perfect. You may even believe that you are the *only* unlucky one on this earth who has been bestowed these unfortunate events.

I have news for you: Everyone—and I do mean *everyone*—is going through (or has been through) something difficult in their lives. Believe it or not, there are even people out there who are going through a lot worse than you are.

This, of course, doesn't change your situation, but sometimes simply knowing this helps shift your perspective and helps you ride the storm with a little more grace and ease.

If you feel as though you want to share your experience and gain support from people who are going through a similar situation, many organizations and communities meet to discuss every possible calamity. These are communities of people who are experiencing (or have experienced) exactly what you are experiencing right now and who meet regularly to support each other. Doing a quick search on the Internet will reveal all the relevant groups in your area. Now, attending such group therapy sessions may not be your cup of tea, but just know that there are many people out there just like you, going through what you are going through right now. There are many more people who have not only been through what you're going through, but have survived, thrived, and bounced back higher than ever!

Sometimes simply knowing this brings a sense of relief and solace. It can be uplifting knowing that that you are not alone.

#4: Create a Circle of Light

When you need support the most, having the "right" people to turn to is fundamental. When I say the word *right* I mean the people who will elevate you, who have your best interests at heart, and who will come from a place of compassion and unconditional love when they advise you. The last thing you need is to be judged, informed "I told you so," or lectured by someone who will add fuel to the fire and destabilize you in your delicate state.

Determining who the right people are can be a little tricky. Sometimes our friends and loved ones say things that are well-intended, but simply don't make us feel any better. For instance, if you are in the middle of a divorce after your spouse cheated on you, you don't need to hear, "I can't believe he did that! What a jerk! You deserve so much better than him!" There is a lot of negativity in those words, and the last thing you need when you are feeling down and out is more negativity.

To find out who are the right people in your life that fall into your "circle of light," simply ask yourself who are the people close to you that make you feel good. Ask yourself, *When I meet with this person, do I feel elevated and happy after leaving, or do I feel drained and demoralized?* Allow your inner feelings to be your guiding compass. Choose people who are great listeners, who do not treat you like a victim, who will not judge you or the people involved, and who have your best interests in mind.

In my case, I had two people in my circle of light: my brother, Tony, and my good friend Cindy Ashton. I knew that if I went to them, they would say the words I needed to hear at that moment. There was never any judgment in their comforting words, and they always came from a place of love. I always felt better after confiding in them.

Sometimes, we don't like reaching out to others because we don't want to be a burden or bring others down, or perhaps we feel the need to protect others who are involved in the situation. I know this was the case with me at first. I felt that I could handle everything on my own, and that it wasn't necessary to concern others or to bring them down too. I also didn't want to reveal to them that my partner was an alcoholic. I knew they were very fond of him and I felt I would be betraying him by letting anyone know this "secret." I wanted to protect him. I kept the situation under wraps until I just couldn't anymore—until I reached the breaking point. I soon realized I couldn't handle everything on my own. I needed support.

When I confided to both Cindy and Tony for the first time, they were both shocked. They had no idea of what I was going through. I guess I had done a great job of hiding it from everyone. They were also disappointed that I had not gone to them earlier.

You may find that, at times, your situation requires support on a different level. Perhaps you need support from people who are also going through (or have been through) what you are going through right now. Your regular friends and/or family may be a great support system for you, but you may need some additional support in an area to which your regular circle of light would not be able to relate, or in which they are not qualified to give you the proper advice or guidance.

For instance, I knew that my circle of light was unable to guide me or advise me in any way on what to do or how to handle being with an alcoholic partner. Alcoholism is a very delicate and serious situation. I had absolutely no idea what to do, what to say, how to behave, or how to handle it. One thing I did know was that I certainly wasn't handling it the right way, because I was at the end of my rope, feeling completely deflated and broken down—and my partner's drinking binges didn't stop. In fact, they actually increased. I knew I needed help with understanding this disease, I needed guidance on what to do, and I needed support to help me deal with the situation, so I attended Al-Anon Meetings (a support group for family and friends of alcoholics). There, I was able to connect with others going through the same difficulty I was, and I gained a better understanding of the disease and how to cope with it.

Creating a circle of light and receiving support is important during challenging times. Choose these people carefully. If you feel that you don't have anyone in your life who could fill those shoes, reach outside of your usual circle. For example, you could confide in a counselor, a community group, a coach, or maybe your pastor or spiritual advisor.

> *Tip*
>
> Take a sheet of paper and write at the top of it, "My Circle of Light." List the people you know who would be good candidates for your special, exclusive group. These are the people you know you can go to when you are about to have a meltdown or just feel the need to talk to someone. Also become keenly aware of the people you consciously did not include on your list. Those are the people you do not want to go to when you need a pick-me-up and require support. Simply becoming aware of who is a part of your "circle of light" and who is not will help you consciously choose who you will go to when you need support the next time.

#5: Learn or Recycle

If you are finding that the same negative things keep happening to you over and over again, and it seems as though you just can't get a break, there may very well be a good reason for this.

When life throws us a curve ball, we are put in a precarious position. We are required to deal with and react to the situation the best we can, and we hope and pray that it is handled well and resolved quickly. But many people are neglecting (or are unaware of) one very important component when handling a difficult situation: They are not doing the inner self-inquiry required regarding what has happened.

In all of what we call "negative" situations, there is a lesson to be learned and growth to be experienced. When we step over and ignore that very important step in our journey, there is a good chance the situation will repeat itself. The situations may end up showing up with different circumstances and different people each time, but the overall experience will be the same. You see, we can run away from our problems and think we have dealt with it. But in reality, we haven't dealt with it at all.

For instance, you may find yourself in a position in which you really hate your job, your coworkers, and your boss, and you view it as a bad situation that you need to do something about. If your solution is to simply find another job and that's it, there's a very good chance that the next job you get will be a miserable experience for you as well.

The same goes for relationships. If you are looking to find your soulmate but yet are finding that this has become quite a difficult search and you are constantly going from relationship to relationship, you have missed something important. Now, you may be chalking up your negative experiences to bad luck, but that isn't the case at all.

You are merely recycling over and over again. You see, there are lessons to be learned and transformational growth to experience within these occurrences, but until you learn and grow, you will find yourself in the same situation over and over again. These lessons and growth are internal in nature and unique to you.

You may have heard the old saying, "Wherever you go, there you are." You can run away all you want from each situation, but if you don't learn the lesson or grow from the experience, you are not changing anything. Sure, the external circumstances may look different, but nothing has really changed. *You* haven't changed, and if *you* haven't changed, neither will your *experience* of everything around you.

Self-inquiry is crucial when we find ourselves in the midst of challenging times. Going inward and doing some self-reflection will help with uncovering what it is you were supposed to learn about yourself and the situation. This is an opportunity for expanding your mind and for tremendous personal growth. It can (and most definitely will) dramatically affect your future experiences in that area in a positive way.

Tip

Sit comfortably in a chair and close your eyes. Take a few deep breaths. Think about the situation you are in and ask yourself this question: "If there is a lesson I am supposed to learn in this situation, what would it be?" Sit with that question for a while and see what comes up for you.

If you find that your answers are directing you to a negative response, then allow that thought to pass through your mind, like clouds moving through the sky, and release it. For instance, if you just got out of a cheating relationship and what comes up for you is "The lesson I was supposed to learn is to never trust men," that is a negatively charged statement with resentment and blame all over it. The lesson you are *supposed* to learn is *not* negative in nature. The lesson you are supposed to learn should make you feel empowered, and a sense of freedom should come over you.

So ask yourself the question again. Keep on asking this question, and when you come up with an answer that lights you up and makes you feel good, that's the lesson. Make sure you write it down.

Chapter 2:
Surrender, Let Go, and Have Faith

*Just trust that everything is unfolding the
way it is supposed to. Don't resist.*

*Surrender to what is, let go of what was,
and have faith in what will be.*

—Sonia Ricotti

#6: Surrender to What Is

I'm sure you've heard of the old saying, "What you resist, persists." The more you resist what is going on in your
life, or judge your situation and believe it should be any
other way, the more you will suffer.

Want to stop or diminish the suffering? Surrender to
your situation. Accept it exactly the way it is. Why should
you accept it the way it is? Because it *is* the way it is. You
can fight it, argue it, cry about it, say it isn't fair, and blame
others all you want, but none of that changes the situation.

Wishing isn't going to change anything. When you resist and fight what "is" in your life, you are adding more pain to your existence.

You can choose to resist what is happening (and many people do), or you can choose to accept it and surrender to it. The journey itself and your experience of it will be dramatically different depending on which choice you make.

Imagine yourself swimming in a river, when you get caught in a powerful current. At that moment you have a choice: You can choose to swim against the current (which no doubt is very tiring, requires a lot of effort, and will probably get you nowhere), or you can choose to float and flow with the current (which is a lot less tiring, and peaceful).

I want to clarify that when I use the term *surrender* I am not saying "give up." What I am saying is stop the chaos in your mind about the situation. Instead of fighting it, saying it shouldn't be happening or should be different, simply accept the situation exactly the way it is. Accept it. It is happening. It is the way it is. (Actually, that's one of my favorite sayings. Anytime I find myself stewing about something that has happened, I always catch myself and say, "Oh well, it is the way it is." And then I let it go.)

This simple act of surrendering to what "is" and not wishing it were any other way (which is futile) will dramatically affect the way you experience your current situation. You are in essence choosing the easier path. What you will find as well is that you will begin to gain more mental clarity when you let go of all the clutter, fog, and negativity in your mind that accompanies resistance. This clarity will help you move forward, find solutions to your problem, and make this experience a lot less painful.

One great example of surrendering to "what is" is explained beautifully in the following true story that happened not long ago. It first began with a conversation between myself and a good friend of mine.

The Conversation

I remember the conversation as if it were yesterday. I don't remember what my friend Melinda and I had been talking about before we got to this part, but I'll always remember these words:

"Sonia, I am going to tell you something, but you have to promise me you are not going to freak out," she said.

"Okay, don't worry," I said. "I won't freak out. What is it?"

"You *have* to promise me you are not going to freak out, okay?" she repeated.

"I promise. Don't worry, I'll be fine. Just tell me," I said impatiently.

"I have breast cancer."

"OH S%#!T!"

My heart sank. I couldn't believe the words I had just heard. *Cancer? How can she have cancer? She is so young. This can't be true.* My heart was beating out of my chest. *Be calm. Be calm. You promised you wouldn't freak out.*

A month later, she was in surgery.

The Surgery

I was with Melinda that day. As I sat next to her bed, waiting for her to wake up, I wrote in my journal. I was amazed at how she was handling everything. This was my journal entry:

Mount Sinai Hospital

August 16, 2010

Wow, I don't even know where to begin. I am feeling really emotional. I'm sitting by Melinda's bedside right now. She had her surgery today. I am amazed; amazed at how positive, happy, and happy-go-lucky she has been. I have never seen anything like it before. She didn't even seem nervous when I picked her up this morning at 6 a.m.

Before going into surgery, she was even jokingly modeling her new wardrobe (hospital attire). With one hand on her hip, in a modeling stance, she asked with a big smile, "So, how do you like my new dress, fancy new shoes, and beautiful hat?"

She was referring to her light blue hospital gown, her plastic slipper covers, and the plastic cap covering her hair. I laughed out loud. I wondered:

How can she be so happy when she is about to get major invasive surgery?

How can she be so happy when she doesn't know how things are going to turn out?

How can she be so happy when she knows she has a year of hell ahead of her?

How can she be so happy when she has cancer?

But somehow she is. She is happy, almost giddy. It is quite surreal actually, even strange. You would think that she has lost her mind. This is not "normal" behavior for someone going through something like this.

Maybe her light-hearted, upbeat, attitude is to appease others, to make others feel "okay" with what's happening.

Well, if that's the case, it worked. I certainly feel better.

A Choice

For a while there I thought Melinda was in denial. Her upbeat and happy attitude seemed odd, and was almost uncomfortable for me. There were times when I wanted to shake her and ask, "What is wrong with you?! Why aren't you freaking out? Don't you see what's happening here?"

Fortunately, I refrained from doing that. I chose to stand back, be supportive, and simply observe instead. As the next few months passed, I watched as Melinda handled the situation. I was in awe. She was not in denial; she knew exactly what was happening.

Here is her story in her own words.

A Message From Melinda Asztalos

Many people would not dare call cancer a gift, but I do. I have come to discover that the scary "C" word is not so scary once you recognize that it can be a powerful tool for transformation, one that really has no limitations.

I watched my mother die painfully and at times quite fearfully from breast cancer, yet in her darkest hour I could still see the light of the human spirit shine, unshakable and immovable. From this observation I would chart a course that I had no idea I would be embarking upon.

On April 3, 2010, I put on a nice, crisp, white T-shirt and noticed a very large mass through my T-shirt on my right breast. I became very still. A thought penetrated the stillness: *What is this?* Another thought answered, *You know exactly what this is.*

As I stared in the mirror peacefully, I thought, *Are you afraid to die?*

No, actually, I am not, it would be like going home.

Immediately with that thought, I looked around at all of the objects in the room and I felt a tremendous sense of relief. *I don't have to worry about this mundane material stuff anymore; the clock, the mirror, the carpet, the phone bill. These are just things to be dealt with, and I do not need to be in a relationship with them the same way anymore.*

Instantly there was great peace around and within me. *I can let go, yet still do what needs to be done. I no longer need to be bound by the fear of situations that come and go in life. My task now is to surrender to what is and to make peace with every moment. From now on, every moment is a choice of creation. Every moment is an opportunity to either expand or contract; the choice is mine.*

In the coming months, I kept my heart open and lived in a state of surrender, paying close attention to the illusion that I was in control of outside events. The only thing I was in absolute control of was my spirit, my connection to inner wisdom, and the moment-to-moment choices I could make. I chose to make jokes, to laugh, and to stay away from people who would see me as a victim.

I began to experiment with what happens when you come from a space of love instead of fear. I noticed that the universe is indeed friendly. Information that I needed came to me easily. Help came to me without reservation or condition, and the world smiled back at me. The stronger the love in my heart grew, the greater my gratitude expanded and allowed me to see cancer as a powerful catalyst for transformation. The more gratitude I felt the more I manifested small miracles.

Of course there were also some dark moments too. There were times when I felt raw and open like a wound, when tears flowed and fear flooded my being. As I stayed present to the pain, not looking for a way to escape, I examined my thoughts and then invited them to leave, replacing them with thoughts of gratitude for my healing, gratitude for receiving guidance, gratitude for the blessings I enjoyed. I remember the day of my surgery. I was scheduled for a bi-lateral mastectomy. I just knew that everything was going to turn out perfectly. I was blessed with a surgeon who was not only incredibly capable, but she also really cared.

I figured, why shouldn't I make this an interesting experience? Why does everything have to be so melodramatic? The situation is what it is, so why not bring humor into it and lighten things up a bit for the people around me? I made jokes with the hospital staff. I kept things light, and the more I did that the easier everything became.

Just before surgery, on the operating table, I sat up and asked for everyone's attention so that I could thank them with heartfelt gratitude and appreciation for assisting me on this journey. I never for a moment felt alone. The surgery went so well that it ended an hour and a half earlier. No complications, no drama, no stress.

Surrendering to my situation and not fighting it (the last thing I want is to be at war with myself) to me means letting go of the illusion that by strictly focusing on doing, you can create a more desirable reality. Surrender is letting go of resistance so you can feel your way to the next step, the next feeling, the next level of being, and the next action to take. It means you are no longer getting in the way of yourself. When you surrender to your situation you are allowing beauty to come into your life, and your experience of this situation shifts dramatically.

Cancer is a physical reality, to be dealt with appropriately, and this can be done fearlessly the more we understand the meaning of surrender and release. Every moment that we can chip away at resistance, we come closer to uncovering the truth that we are active participants of our unique journey.

I am a willing participant in my destiny, and I claim my well-being. As I continue to move forward with chemotherapy treatments, I have committed to listening to my inner spirit and following my inner guidance. I am open to opportunity and I am mindful of the messages and miracles that continue to come my way.

Sometimes miracles and opportunities come in strange packages—you've got to open the package and explore. Every moment of every day is an opportunity to make a choice. I choose gratitude. I choose life. I choose appreciation. I choose fearlessness. I choose me.

I am truly in awe of how Melinda chose to handle her situation. She could have chosen to feel sorry for herself, panic, be angry, feel sad, and simply be mad at the world. Many people *do* choose that when faced with such a traumatic experience, and they often remain stuck there for a very long time (sometimes forever). I'm sure that those emotions *have* come up a few times here and there for her, but ultimately she chose to surrender to what *is*. This choice made all the difference in how she experienced the events happening in her life and made the journey for the people around her who love and care for her a lot easier to handle.

Stop resisting and judging what "is" in your life. When you resist and judge, you will only experience more pain and suffering. By accepting it, you release it, and you will stumble upon the light.

Tip

The next time you feel angry, hurt, or frustrated, become aware of those feelings. Ask yourself, *What am I resisting here? What is it that I am judging?* Let the answers come to you. Then consciously release it. Accept the situation the way it is right now and let go of the negative thoughts around it.

#7: Let Go of What Was

It's time to turn the page and move forward. I mean *really* move forward. Don't dog-ear the page and *then* turn it, but move forward without looking back. The past is history. It no longer exists, but you are keeping it alive in your mind through your thoughts. Let it go. It is not serving you.

Holding on to the negative events of the past and wishing things were different or dwelling on what happened is *not* going to change the past. Nothing is going to change the past. However, if you are holding on to your past and keeping it alive in your mind (as if it is still happening), it will dramatically affect your present, and, inevitably, your future.

You see, holding on to the past is like walking around with an invisible anchor attached to your leg. Wherever you go, there it is. So although you are currently living in the present, your past is always being dragged around with you. It is there whenever you need to make a decision, whenever something happens and you react—it is right there affecting every move you make.

For instance, as I mention in *The Law of Attraction Plain and Simple*, if you were cheated on in a previous relationship and you were deeply hurt and scarred from that situation, there is a very good chance that the next time you meet someone, you will be worried, concerned, or perhaps even close your heart off to love altogether. This not only affects your present, but ultimately it will affect your future as well. It is in your best interest to let go of what "was" if you wish to move forward and bounce back higher than ever.

Decide Which Direction to Take

When a traumatic event occurs in our lives, we have a choice to make: Do we suffer through it all and quickly run back to safety and the way it was, or do we awaken and open our hearts and souls to a new life—a new, awakened way of being?

All the people I have spoken to who have bounced back higher than ever after a crisis have let go of their past and moved forward into a new life. They didn't hold on to what *was*. They didn't spend their time worrying and dwelling on how it used to be and wishing it was the way it was before. They embraced their new lives and moved forward with confidence, peace, and excitement for what *will* be.

The way I see it, when a crisis happens in your life, you have three journeys you can take:

1. You can choose to take the *safe journey* and simply do whatever it takes to get through it—"ride the storm," so to speak—and run back to your old way of living and thinking. You run to the safety zone and hope and pray that you don't ever have to experience or suffer such pain again. The safety zone isn't always the most fulfilling place to be. Sometimes it is quite mundane and purposeless, and often feelings of unhappiness and emptiness creep in, but it is safe.

2. You can choose to take the *awakened journey*. You leave the past behind you, let go of what was, learn, grow, look for the silver lining, and move forward

into the unknown and into a new, awakened world; a rebirth of sorts. This is where miracles occur and where a new and fulfilling life is lived.

3. You can choose to take the *in-between journey*. You suffer through the calamity, ride the storm, and then, instead of running all the way back to your old life, you run only halfway and sit on a fence. When this happens, you are stuck between two worlds: the *safe* world and the new *awakened* world. In other words, you want to take the leap to the awakened world, but fear is holding you back and your safe world is calling you (even though, at a deeper, intuitive level, you know this is not the world you wish to return to). The *in-between journey* is probably the most confusing and difficult journey of all. When you are stuck on the *in-between journey* there is a lot of confusion and fear.

I find that many people I meet in my workshops fall into this third category. They know they want to make a change in their lives, and they don't want to return to the way it was, but they are having difficulty and are unsure of what steps to take to move in the direction of this new awakened world. In fact, they are usually attending my workshop to seek guidance of some sort (or perhaps to be given a nudge) to help them move toward that new world.

There are many reasons why people choose to sit on that fence. The main reason, however, is fear. Fear of letting go of the past (and the known), fear of the unknown, fear of making a mistake, fear of what others will think, fear of looking stupid, and even fear of success! All those fears you have that are stopping you, the reasons why you are choosing to not make that move to let go of your past and move toward a greater life, are all a feeble attempt at controlling your external world.

Let me say one very important thing here: Fear is normal. Everyone experiences fear. You can't make fear simply go away, but what you can do is shift your relationship with your fear. Instead of retreating when you feel fearful, feel excited. When you feel fear, instead of backing away, move toward it. When you do, you are moving toward a new awakened life.

I remember a while back I had met a man at the red carpet movie premiere of *Tapping the Source* in Los Angeles. We were both featured teachers in the movie. I had never heard of him before, but when I saw him in the movie and then met him after the premiere, I was in awe. There were 115 teachers in that movie, and most of them were very well-known in the self-help industry, but Sam really captured my heart—not only because of his story (which will be told shortly), but also because of his incredible heart, constant smile, and his wonderful zest for life. When you meet someone like that, it is always a gift, but what made him even more incredible was the fact that he retained his optimism even after the most tragic event occurred in his life. He is a perfect example of someone who has chosen the awakened journey, someone who has consciously chosen to let go of what was and embraced and embarked on a new calling and a new life.

It was very obvious by merely looking at this young, handsome man that something had happened to him: He has a prosthetic right arm and he walks with a limp. Those physical cues are just two small symbols of what he has been through. In fact, this man is a walking miracle. In October 2006, this man, Sam Cawthorn, died, and lived to tell about it.

SAM CAWTHORN'S STORY

I remember it as if it was yesterday. It was October 3, 2006. I was 26 years old. I was a Youth Futurist for the Australian federal government, and was also a professional hip-hop dancer, a professional musician, and was involved in many theater productions.

I was driving on the highway when it happened: I fell asleep at the wheel. I was going more than 100 kilometers an hour [about 62 mph] when I had a head-on collision with a tractor-trailer that was also going more than 100 kilometers an hour.

The impact woke me up. I remember sitting there in the car, fighting for every single breath. Some people had stopped to help me. I remember they were holding my head up and asking me questions about my family and my life. They wanted to keep me alert. I just wanted to go to sleep.

I lost consciousness. I stopped breathing. My heart stopped.

On October 3, 2006, at 3:06 p.m., I died. Shortly thereafter, the paramedics managed to resuscitate me. I was put in an ambulance, and off to the hospital I went. I was put on life support and was in a coma for six days.

The entire right side of my body was in pieces. My right (and dominant) arm was ripped off my shoulder during the accident. My right leg was a mess. I left part of my quadricep (upper thigh) on the highway. I also broke and lost a part of my femur, and lost my kneecap. I broke my fibula, my ankle, and six ribs. I had a lacerated liver, a punctured kidney, and both my lungs were collapsing at the same time. I lost all my blood twice-over in the first 12 hours of the accident.

I was told by the doctor that I would never walk again. That although I was a professional hip hop dancer, I would never dance again. That although I was a professional musician, I would never play the guitar again. That although I have two little daughters, I would never walk them down the aisle on their wedding day.

Two days after coming out of my coma, I was in a state of denial. I remember thinking, *This has not happened to me. This is just a nightmare and I'm going to wake up soon.*

I had to eventually accept my situation. Once I did, I cried for about a week. I went through pillow after pillow just from my tears. I released all my mental anguish. It was a really hard time for me. I was in the hospital for five months and in a wheelchair for a year.

I believe that when a massive adversity or problem occurs there is something deep down within each of us, a driving inner strength, that sometimes we don't even realize we have, until such a time arrives. The consistent thought that entered my mind was, "I'm going to prove you wrong."

My rehabilitation was really difficult. I had all these metal fixators all over my leg, and my arm was aching from phantom pains. I went through several surgeries and rehabilitation every single day for five or six hours a day.

It was a tough time, but again, there was a driving spirit within me that was saying, "I'm going to do this."

The community I had around me was incredible. My wife was absolutely amazing. She was a solid rock for me. My children, my brothers and sisters, my mom and dad, my work colleagues—all their support helped me get through it. My very strong faith in a greater being helped me as well. I knew that I could not get through my accident by myself and that I needed to draw from a higher power.

After being in a wheelchair for a year, I managed to pick myself up the same exact day a year after my accident. I got rid of my wheelchair that day. From the day I began walking again, I made the decision not to look back. I decided not to go back to the place I was before my accident because there was something new in my life, there was something different. Something had shifted. Something had changed in my life, beyond my obvious physical disability. *I* had also changed emotionally and mentally. I knew I had a new purpose—a new calling.

Shortly thereafter, I was asked to speak about my experience at a local church. Normally there are about 300 people who attend this church, the day I spoke, there were almost 1,000 people who attended. From there, everything catapulted and schools and businesses everywhere were asking me to speak. Today, I get to travel all over the world speaking for major multi-national organizations.

Opportunity comes when you continually push forward. When you hit rock bottom—and we all do at some point in our lives—focus on bouncing out of that situation and continually move forward in your life. To me, success is not what you do when you are on top. Success is how high you bounce when you hit the bottom.

If I would have listened to the doctors, I would still be in a wheelchair today. If I did not have that fighting inner strength (that I think we all have), I would still be in a wheelchair today. But here I am. Yes, I lost my dominant arm above the elbow. Yes, my right leg doesn't bend at all, so it is hard for me to sit in a chair, in a car, in a theater, or in a plane. I will never be able to ride a bike, and I'll never be able to go for a jog, but I believe in focusing on the good things in life—hey, I get disability [handicapped] spots now!

First and foremost, I'm alive! I now have a new and incredible life with a purpose, which I absolutely love!

What I love about Sam's story is that after his tragic event occurred, he never wanted to go back to his old life; he instead chose to embrace a new one.

He was once asked in a radio interview, "If you had the opportunity to change what happened on that fateful day in October on that highway, would you?" His response was shocking. He said, "No, I wouldn't change a thing because if that event hadn't happened, I wouldn't be the person I am today."

Now, I would say that Sam Cawthorn is the ultimate example of letting go of what was.

#8: Have Faith in What Will Be

Faith is an interesting word. When I researched it in various dictionaries, I found that it has many meanings and definitions. I have also found that it means different things to different people . To some, *faith* is a religious term; to others it represents hope and belief in something, but regardless of what the word means to you, faith can offer comfort when you are faced with challenging experiences.

I found my favorite definition of the word in the English World Dictionary:

Faith: A strong or unshakeable belief in something, especially without proof or evidence.

An "unshakeable belief"—those words really ring true to me; believing in something beyond a shadow of a doubt.

Faith is what I had when everything in my life felt as though it was falling apart. Without it, I'm not sure how I would have gotten through everything. Believing in something bigger than myself, believing that everything was happening for a reason, believing that everything was going to be okay, believing that something incredible was going to come out of it is what helped me move from the deep darkness toward the light.

I have interviewed many people who have transcended their challenging ordeals, and I noticed that they all talked about how they had faith and believed in a higher power. For many, it was God; for others, it was Buddha; for still others it was "Source" or "the Universe." It doesn't matter what you call it or what you believe in, having faith that all will be well, that all is unfolding perfectly and as it is supposed to is a powerful place to come from.

Think of a time in the past when something major happened in your life when you thought it was the worst thing that could possibly have happened. Then, a month, a year, or two years later you realized it was the best thing that ever happened to you.

It may not be clear right now why things are happening the way they are. But having faith and trust that it is all unfolding as it is supposed to can have a calming effect when you are in the midst of a chaotic storm. Have faith that it is all unfolding for a higher purpose. Be patient. The purpose will reveal itself with time—if you allow it to.

My good friend Janet Bray Attwood, *New York Times* best-selling coauthor of *The Passion Test*, has a great personal story that reflects and demonstrates the importance of letting go and trusting the universe. Here is her story.

THE GIFT IS ALWAYS THERE— JANET BRAY ATTWOOD

Letting go and trusting in the universe is probably the all-time greatest challenge anyone can face. Walking in the dark with total blind faith, not knowing where the next safe footing will be, afraid that the unknown will unveil more than we can handle, is never easy. Especially when life seems to be offering up one intense challenge after another.

One of my first experiences of consciously letting go and handing it all over to the universe was in 1983. I was in a job recruiting disk-drive engineers in Silicon Valley, and was failing miserably. Luckily for me, one day after work when I was meditating in the local meditation center, I opened my eyes and noticed a poster on the bulletin board advertising a success seminar to be held in San Francisco the following weekend. I had been praying for a sign as to what my gifts were, and the moment I glanced at the poster on the wall, I knew that somehow my prayers had been answered.

My intuition couldn't have been more on! Not only did I take the seminar, but I also realized while there that what I wanted to do more than anything was to be a great transformational leader. I eventually persuaded the seminar leader of that program, Debra Poneman, to hire me and teach me how to be a trainer of her program, "Yes to Success."

It turned out that Debra was going on her U.S. speaking tour at about the same time I was to arrive in Los Angeles, where her company was located. Debra said I could stay in her apartment and study her success tapes while she was on tour, and when she returned, I could start my illustrious career, uplifting and speaking to hundreds, maybe even thousands of people all over the world.

I was in seventh heaven!

Two weeks later, after Debra and I finalized our plans, I happily said goodbye to all of my friends at the recruiting firm, packed my bags, filled my vintage red Toyota up with gas and headed down to Los Angeles, radio blaring, singing at the top of my lungs, ecstatic that I was on the way to starting my dream career.

Two miles into my journey my little red Toyota started sputtering and spurting. Steam started rising up over the front of my car from inside the hood, and as I was pulling over to the side of the freeway to see what was going on, my trusty little red car took one big breath, let out the most God-awful sound, and died right there on the freeway.

I was stunned and horrified by what had just happened, and plump little tears started to form in my eyes. After the initial shock of saying farewell to my beloved Toyota, I paid the man who came to tow my car away an additional $50 to drop me off at the train station. After paying him, buying my train ticket to Los Angeles, and then taking a ridiculously long taxi ride to Debra's apartment in Santa Monica from the train station, to my horror, shame, dismay, and anxiety, I arrived at Debra's door with $13 to my name.

Frozen with fear that Debra wouldn't hire me if she knew I was completely broke, I pretended that everything was A-okay and said nothing while we were together. Instead I acted like a woman in control and kept a rather frozen imitation of a sunny smile on my face until Debra finally waved goodbye to me.

Now what am I going to do?! I asked myself. Totally freaked out by the fact that I hardly had enough money to last me more than a day, I went to Debra's refrigerator and scooped myself a huge serving of her chocolate ice cream. After eating almost the whole half gallon, I laid down on her couch and fell into a chocolate-drunken sleep.

When I awoke, I summoned up all the courage I could muster and decided there was only one option when things got this bad.

I grabbed the keys to Debra's blue Chevy, which she had said I could borrow if I needed it, although I only wanted to put on miles if there was an emergency (and this definitely spelled E-M-E-R-G-E-N-C-Y). So with my heart pounding and my knees shaking, I sped down the Pacific Coast Highway, full of dread yet excited at what I was going to do, knowing that it would definitely seal my fate, for better or worse!

Ten minutes later I arrived at my destination. I pulled Debra's car into the parking lot of the great Saint Paramahansa Yogananda's Self-Realization Fellowship Center. I had visited this place many times before, and it always gave me the same incredible feeling of peace. Once again, I immediately felt a deep sense of calm take over me. I walked past all of the beautiful buildings to the majestic and serene gardens that graced this special place, and reached into my purse and nervously pulled out every one of my treasured one-dollar bills. One by one I carefully stuffed each dollar bill into one of the little tin donation boxes that were strategically placed in and around the gardens.

When I had donated all that I had, I sat down on a nearby wooden bench and had a very intimate talk with God, pouring out my heart and telling him all that was going on with me and where I could use a little of his support.

After a little while, I walked back to Debra's blue Chevy and headed back down the highway to her apartment. Once in the car a huge flash of reality immediately set in.

"What the hell did you just do?! Are you craaaazy?" I asked myself out loud.

Gripping the steering wheel as if trying to gain some sense of control, I sped faster down the highway, continuing to talk to myself out loud.

"Perfect! Good one! Brilliant! The car is almost out of gas, you have no food in the fridge, and you decide to be a spiritual mood-maker with your last 13 dollars?! Way to go! Oh yeah, you're gonna make one helluva transformational leader! Augh!!!"

Depressed and dejected, I pulled up to Debra's apartment. The minute I walked in the front door the phone rang. In my most tortured voice, holding back my tears, I managed to squeak out a very weak "Hullo?"

"Janet, is that you?"

"Uh huh, who's this?" I asked, wishing whomever it was would somehow vanish.

"It's me, Francis."

Francis was my ex-husband's father, whom I loved and hadn't heard from in more than a year.

"Hi Francis, it's so nice to hear from you! How are you? Wow, how did you find me?" I asked, and immediately I started to feel a wave of relief come over me. Francis always had that effect on me. After we chatted on the phone for some time, Francis persuaded me to meet him for lunch at a nearby restaurant. "My treat," he said.

At the restaurant, Francis was very animated and talking 100 miles a minute. He had just started selling what he considered the best natural weight-loss program on the market. As he was telling me all these amazing things about the product, he put four bottles of it on the table and said, "I think this is something you could really make a lot of money on in your spare time. Are you in?"

"The opportunity sounds great," I said. "How about when I have a little more extra cash, I'll order some from you?"

Without missing a beat, Francis continued, "I just happen to have $500 worth of the stuff in the trunk of my car I brought just for you! You can have these bottles on the table and the $500 worth as well. Pay me back after you sell it and make some money for both of us."

Francis immediately handed me his four bottles, and at that exact moment, a very overweight waitress walked up to our table, looked straight at the bottles, and asked, "What's that?"

Trying my best to remember what Francis had just shared about the weight-loss product, I started telling her in my most authoritative voice all it could do.

"Does this stuff really work?" she asked, looking first at Francis and then at me.

"I just dropped 50 pounds from this product," Francis beamed. "Best of all," he said, "I never felt hungry."

"I'm just starting it today," I added.

"Well, I hope it does the same for me!" the waitress said, smiling as she scanned Francis's lean physique. She then whipped out five of the most beautiful $20 bills from under her apron and slapped them on the table. "How much do I owe you?" she asked, grabbing the four bottles.

"It comes to $101.97 with the tax, but considering you're our first customer of the day, we'll let you have the four bottles for $100" Francis said.

"Hope it works!" the waitress said.

"That's yours," Francis said, indicating the waitress's 20s. "Good job! Yup, you're going to do just fine with this!"

Stunned and overjoyed that I now had $100 in my pocket, I walked out to Francis's car and loaded up Debra's Chevy with rest of the product he had brought with him. As Francis pulled out of the parking lot I remembered the $13 I had just donated earlier in the day. A big smile came over my face as I realized once again how magical the universe is.

This experience was a profound reminder for me, and one I've remembered often in the 28 years since these events took place. Donating my last $13 helped me to remember that we are always taken care of. The support may come in strange and mysterious ways, but when we stay open to what is appearing now, the gift is always there.

I love Janet's story because it is a reminder that sometimes we don't know how things are going to turn around.

There are times when we can't predict or even fathom a possible scenario in our minds of how it will happen, but it doesn't matter. It will. Somehow, it will.

It isn't always easy to have faith when everything around you is falling apart, but trust, simply trust that all is unfolding with exact precision. Let go of the resistance, surrender to what is, and believe with every fiber in your body that it is all unfolding for the betterment of your highest good. And of course, be open to what shows up in front of you. It may not make sense to you at all right now; that's okay. It will. With time.

Chapter 3:
Master Your Mind

A happy life consists in tranquility of mind.
—Cicero

#9: Re-Create Your Reality

Often we get so caught up in what is happening outside of us that we believe the way we are feeling is the result of these external circumstances. This isn't true. That belief is all an illusion. For instance, let's say your boss just yelled at you, and your reaction is anger and frustration. You may believe you are feeling those negative feelings because your boss just yelled at you. However, there is a missing component here. There is something that occurs between how your boss behaved toward you and your feelings after it happens. What is it that occurs? You have a thought.

That thought you had the moment after your boss yelled at you is what caused you to feel angry and frustrated. It isn't his actual yelling at you that caused those negative feelings, but rather what you chose to make it mean and what you said to yourself at that moment. It all happens in a split second.

"What is causing you pain?" I often ask in my workshops. Inevitably, people's responses always veer toward their circumstances.

"My husband has left me for another woman."

"My son is an addict, and I don't know what to do anymore."

"I have serious financial problems."

"I have a serious health issue."

Most people are unable to separate their circumstances from their feelings. They truly believe they feel those negative feelings *because of* their circumstances. They believe their circumstances are the *cause* of their suffering and pain. That isn't true.

What's causing your suffering and pain is not the circumstances you are in, but *your thoughts about* the circumstances you are in. Your *thinking* is what is causing your pain. This statement is true in *all* situations.

Your perception and interpretation of the situation is creating your current reality. If the perception you chose and interpretation you created is not making you feel good, then change it. That's right, change it. Shift your thoughts about it. Change your interpretation and perception of what "is" to a more positive one and you'll be amazed at what happens.

Now, you may be thinking this is easier said than done, but it really isn't that hard. First, by simply becoming aware of your thoughts you immediately have the ability to consciously change them. That is the first step in shifting how you feel. Whenever you aren't feeling good, simply become consciously aware of your thinking. What are your thoughts at that moment? Then, analyze them. Ask yourself, *Is there a different way I can be thinking of this situation?*

Recognize that what you think is happening or has happened is *not* what really happened. It is your *interpretation* of what happened. You chose to make it mean what it did, and if the choice you made isn't making you feel very good, then change it! You have control over how you feel. There are many different interpretations to every single situation; if the one you chose makes you angry, sad, and frustrated, then you need to choose a different interpretation. Begin examining different scenarios in your mind and see how you feel. Once you get to a scenario that makes you smile and feel better, stick to that thought and that interpretation.

Let's go back to the original example of your boss yelling at you. Perhaps you were feeling angry and frustrated because you feel that he was disrespectful toward you, that he is unappreciative of your hard work, and that he thinks he is better than you. That was your interpretation and those were the thoughts you came up with after he yelled at you, which made you feel the way you do. That is what you chose to make it mean.

Of course, we don't know if that is really true. For all we know, your boss had a really bad day. Perhaps *his* boss yelled at *him* and even threatened to fire him. Perhaps he is experiencing some trouble at home and his wife told him that morning that she was leaving him. We can make up so many scenarios around why he yelled at you, and none of them have anything to do with you—except you happened to be in the wrong place at the wrong time, when he felt the need to vent his anger.

The funny thing is that you don't even have to make up any interpretation at all. You can simply let it go and not allow what happened to rent space in your mind. You can choose to not let the circumstance mean anything at all, and release it.

Rediscover What Is Possible

My good friend Gina Mollicone-Long, best-selling author of *Think or Sink*, has recently shared with me a great way to shift your thinking, especially when you are stuck, overwhelmed, and feel like you have a mountain in front of you. Sometimes we get in our own way by putting restrictions and constraints on ourselves about what is possible. It is time to remove the *IM* from *impossible* and begin creating and doing things that you never even dreamed were possible. Here is Gina's story.

TAKING THE "IM" OUT OF IMPOSSIBLE— GINA MOLLICONE-LONG

I'd like to share with you a technique that is very powerful for shifting thoughts and energy.

The mind tends to divide the world into things that are possible and things that are impossible. If we conform to these constraints, we are limiting ourselves as to what we can achieve. If you are feeling particularly stuck, a great way to get moving is to pick something that is imPOSSIBLE to do, and then do it. Once you have achieved "the imPOSSIBLE," you are free to explore what other things might also be possible. When you blur the edges of what is possible, you can begin to redefine your reality.

I developed this technique at a time in my life when I was feeling quite stuck in my own limits. After having two children very close together, I reached a point at which my circumstances were more than I could handle. I was used to being good at everything in my life. I was used to mastering my reality. Motherhood was a big wake-up call for me. I felt completely inadequate and there was no training manual in sight. Being good at motherhood was beginning to look more and more impossible every day, so I decided to randomly pick something from my imPOSSIBLE category and take on the challenge of achieving it. I desperately needed to do something that would break the pattern that I had created in my life. I knew that if I could achieve something from the imPOSSIBLE list I could re-create my entire experience.

I chose running a marathon. This is not earth-shattering for many people. But if you knew me, you would understand just how impossible it really was. Believe me when I tell you that I am not a marathoner, and finishing one was less likely than pigs flying. At best, I am a slow walker. But I run because I love to run; I love to feel the wind in my hair and the continuous meditative rhythm of my feet hitting the ground. I became a marathoner in the moment that I decided to do it. I soon filled my days with training and visualizations.

The actual race provided me with one of those insightful, life-changing moments after which things are never the same again. As an expert in peak performance and self-development, I pray for moments like the one I had in my marathon. When I "hit the wall" in that race, I finally understood what it meant to be the *source* of my own angst, and that a shift in my own beliefs and energy was all that was needed to overcome even the most insurmountable obstacles. My ego dissolved the instant I realized that finishing that race came down to one choice I had to make about myself. In choosing to believe in myself, I was able to overcome all the physical challenges that had doomed my race minutes earlier. At the moment I crossed that finish line, I knew I had shifted my energy to a completely different level.

I triumphantly crossed the finish line at 6 hours and 9 minutes. Although I didn't break any world records with that time, I was ecstatic!

You see, there was a particularly dark part of the race for me when I almost gave up. I didn't think I could finish. But in that darkest moment I learned what I was really made of. I learned to believe in myself for the first time in my adult life. I learned to choose happiness regardless of what was happening to me.

Finishing that race was one of the greatest things that ever happened to me because I finally learned to let go of my attachments. It's all about the meaning attached to the result. For me, the meaning was powerful, so the result was powerful. It was a choice I made the moment I decided to finish that race no matter what it took, no matter what it looked like. I chose to be happy well before I crossed the finish line, and it was the most invigorating experience of my life. I chose happiness *first*. This was a change on the inside. As soon as I changed on the inside, the outside immediately followed suit, and the results reflected this change exactly.

Consider that *NOT getting what you want is exactly what you need*. It doesn't matter what you get in life; your happiness doesn't depend on it. You get what you get and that's the way it is. Everything that happens in your life is perfect for you. It couldn't be any other way. Any failure is merely feedback about what's happening on the inside. Failure contains all the clues necessary for you to learn what is standing in your way. Failure is actually a gift, a built-in mechanism that contains all the answers you are looking for.

How many times have you heard, "In hindsight, that [devastating thing] was the greatest thing that ever happened to me"? For example, you really needed to leave for work on time because you had a huge sales meeting, but your children needed extra attention in the morning so you were late for work. Because you were late leaving the house, you missed being in a huge multi-car pileup on the freeway. Has this ever happened to you? How many times have you looked back on something with a new perspective and been happy that it turned out the way it did? This occurs all the time.

Instead of relegating this experience to hindsight, I'd like to suggest that you can trust in the wisdom of what is happening *as it happens*. This will allow you to leverage the power of the experience such that you will be able to use it to your advantage immediately, instead of waiting for some vague time in the future when it will finally make sense. There are no accidents in the universe. Everything happens exactly as it should based on your choices every single day. It couldn't be any other way.

We attract what we think about and expect. Failure is an indication that something didn't work. There was a disconnect in the attraction process that led to an unwanted result. By understanding this concept, you can harness the lesson that exists in every single outcome you generate. Where did the disconnect occur? Was it in your choice about who you were being or was it in your actions? Were you consistent with your higher purpose? Were you being who you really are or were you trying to be someone else? Only you know for sure, and the only way to learn is to try. Remember, the first time you try to use failure will be the hardest, but if you persist, you can become a master at directing your life—simply by paying attention to the clues being reflected to you.

Failing is the greatest thing that can happen to you, *if* you learn to use it, *if* you learn to read it and act on it. The key to really leveraging failure is realizing that you have to change something on the inside in order for your outer-world results to change. If you don't, you are simply doing the same thing over and over again, expecting different results. This will drive you crazy. To get something different, you have to try something different. The best way to decide what to do differently is to pay attention to your feedback—your failure—and then make a change on the inside. Hey, with this perspective, you just might find that failing is actually fun!

Another possibility is that you might begin to enjoy the process of living your life now, instead of waiting for something to happen "out there" before you love life. You might start to see that "going for it" is just as much fun, if not *more* fun than "getting it." You might begin to notice the little nuggets of joy that exist everywhere in the present moment. As you become more aware of being happy in the present, you will finally be free to notice the little things in life that really matter. By shifting your focus from lack to abundance and gratitude, you allow yourself to expand, grow, and live.

Take what is imPOSSIBLE for you and *do it.* Then start knocking off all the other things that used to be imPOSSIBLE and aren't anymore. Once you deconstruct the division between imPOSSIBLE and POSSIBLE, you will have shifted your energy to a new level, never to return again.

Tip

The next time you find yourself feeling angry, sad, frustrated, or hurt, ask yourself this question: What am I thinking right now? It's important to do some self-inquiry and question your thoughts at that moment. What you are thinking about is what is causing you to feel this way. Once you have determined what you were thinking (there is a good chance your past is creeping up on you here), then consciously decide to change your interpretation of what happened (or the situation), and change your thoughts about it.

#10: Shed Your Limiting Beliefs

Everyone harbors limiting beliefs deep within themselves that do not serve us, are negative in nature, and hold us back in life—often without us even knowing it. They hinder us when making decisions during challenging times, prolong our suffering, and prevent us from achieving our true potential.

These beliefs are about ourselves, others, relationships, money, and life itself. For example, here are few that come up often:

- I'm not good enough.
- I'm not smart enough.
- I don't have enough time.
- There's never enough money.
- Life is hard.
- I will never be happy.
- I am not lovable.
- I will never find my soulmate.
- I don't have enough education.
- Rich people are greedy and self-centered.
- I'm too old to make changes in my life now.
- I'll always be broke.
- No one cares about me.
- You have to work hard on a relationship for it to work.

Often we don't even realize we have those beliefs; many are being harbored at a subconscious level.

Beliefs are merely an interpretation of the world based on the evidence you have observed and experienced throughout your life. Your beliefs have been programmed into your mind since early childhood and continue to be programmed into you even today. Our parents, our friends, our teachers, the media, and our own experiences have helped mold and develop our beliefs, which affect our decisions and how we feel, and are a paramount reason for some of the undesirable situations in our lives.

It is important to shed these beliefs that limit us. Holding on to them will prevent you from moving forward and coming out on top.

For instance, if you have been holding on to the belief that rich people are greedy and self-centered, then the chances of actually experiencing financial abundance in your life are slim. You may want to become rich, but if you are harboring that limiting belief in your subconscious mind, it will be virtually impossible to achieve such financial freedom. Why? Because at a deeper level you are inadvertently sabotaging yourself along the way. So, if you are currently in a difficult and challenging financial situation, it is crucial that you uncover what your limiting beliefs are about money and consciously shift them.

Identify Your Limiting Beliefs

It isn't always obvious what your limiting beliefs are, especially if they are held at a subconscious level. Making a conscious effort to identify them will help you uncover them. Once you do, you can work on eliminating them and replacing them with empowering beliefs.

You may be asking yourself, *How can I figure out if I am holding limiting beliefs, and if I am, what are they?* First begin by evaluating the areas in your life that are not working right now or where you are experiencing difficulty (for instance, health, finances, relationships, career, and so on). I can assure you that you have limiting beliefs that are stopping you from being the best you can be in those areas. To unveil them, you will have to begin paying attention to your inner self-talk. The more you become conscious of this inner conversation, the more you will notice the way certain negative thoughts are repeated over and over again. Those are limiting beliefs.

For instance, if you are in a bad relationship and you are choosing to stay in that relationship even if you are unhappy, there is definitely a limiting belief around that. Perhaps you believe (either consciously or subconsciously) that "I'll never meet another man at my age," or maybe, "Who is going to want me? Look at how I let myself go," or maybe, "I'm not a good person; no one will want me." Those limiting beliefs are what is stopping you from moving forward.

Once you have identified your limiting beliefs, you can begin to shed them by proving those statements wrong. Look for evidence that proves them wrong. If you look for it, you will find it. So if "I'll never meet another man at my age" is your limiting belief, look around you for proof of people who have found new and lasting love later in life. There are many all around you! Simply identifying this limiting belief and knowing it isn't true will help you release it; then you can focus on replacing it with an empowering new belief, such as, "I can meet a wonderful man at any age!" This new belief will help you move forward with your life in a positive and empowered way.

Often, when we think of these limiting beliefs, we know that they aren't true and that they are illogical, but somehow they manage to get stuck in our subconscious minds and still affect our thoughts; this of course affects our feelings, which ultimately affects our decisions and whether we take action or not in our lives.

By becoming aware of these limiting beliefs, then recognizing when they come up, consciously releasing them, and replacing them with empowering beliefs instead, you will notice dramatic positive shifts in your life.

Tip

Identify your limiting beliefs, shed them, and replace them with empowering new beliefs.

1. Begin by becoming consciously aware of your inner self-talk. Throughout the next week, notice what you are constantly saying to yourself and jot down the negative statements (beliefs) you say over and over again.

2. Then, next to each belief write what area of your life each statement refers to (career, finances, relationships, health, and so on). You may notice a trend that the most negative beliefs are in the

area of your life in which you are experiencing the most difficulty.

3. Take each belief and search for evidence to disprove it.

4. Shift each of those limiting beliefs into a positive belief.

5. Write out all the positive new beliefs you have created on a separate sheet of paper. These are your new empowering beliefs.

6. Each time you catch yourself thinking one of those negative limiting beliefs, acknowledge it, and then say "cancel" in your mind and replace it with your new positive belief.

It may take time to reprogram your mind to believe these new empowering beliefs, but be patient. What you focus on expands, so the more you focus on these new beliefs, the more they will become your new way of thinking, and you will begin to experience positive shifts in your life.

#11: Step Away From the Closed Door

When you focus on the negative side of things and allow yourself to remain in that pessimistic rut, you are staring at what I call the proverbial closed door. You are not moving forward or changing your situation. In fact, you are not going anywhere at all, and you are prolonging the agony and the pain.

Anytime you blame others and complain about your situation, you are choosing to be a victim. By playing the victim role you are putting yourself in an ineffective and weak position. It is virtually impossible to allow incredible miracles to enter your life when you choose to remain in this negative mental state. So if you realize you are staring at a closed door, consciously choose to step away from it.

Look for the Open Doors All Around You

Begin to consciously shift your thoughts and focus on the positive side of your situation. It may not be an easy task, but if you dig deep enough, you will find it. By doing so, you will automatically walk away from the closed door and begin noticing all the incredible open doors all around you.

Those open doors are doors of opportunity. What's even more incredible is that those "open doors" were *always* there. You were just too busy focusing on the closed door to notice them.

I have a personal story to share with you that demonstrates how consciously stepping away from that proverbial closed door can dramatically change your life. I call it my "Oprah" story.

My "Oprah" Story

Several years ago, I made a commitment to speak at a national health-club conference in Chicago. I was scheduled to speak about Low Cost and No Cost Marketing Ideas. By that time, I had already started my new company, Lead Out Loud, and had written my first book (which was self-published) called *Mastering the Law of Attraction.*

I had committed to speaking at that conference a year earlier, long before I had embarked on this new life-transforming venture. Now, the last thing I wanted to do was go and speak to people about "marketing ideas." All I wanted to do was inspire people to live their greatest lives!

I was not very happy about the whole situation.

The conversation in my head (and even to my friends and family members) went something like this: *How did I get myself into this situation? "Low Cost and No Cost Marketing Ideas"? Are you kidding me? Who wants to talk about that? I can't believe I have to go to Chicago again—and for three days. I am a busy woman. I can't afford to lose three days of my life. How can I get out of this? Maybe I'll call in sick. Maybe I'll tell them I missed my flight.*

I dreaded the thought of going to this conference. Needless to say, I was staring at a closed door.

Then, I remember thinking to myself, *Wow, Sonia, for someone who is always talking about the importance of being positive, you are certainly being negative!* I immediately became aware of how I had interpreted the situation in a negative way and how my thoughts about the situation were negatively affecting how I was feeling. I knew it was important for me to re-create my reality and shift my thoughts. So I did.

I decided at that very moment that not only was I going to go to Chicago and do a great job speaking at the conference, but I was also going to make this trip the best trip I have ever taken in my life! At that moment, I stepped away from the closed door. Of course, I didn't know how I was going to do all of that yet, but I knew everything would fall into place beautifully somehow.

I started to think of what I could possibly do in Chicago that would make me happy and turn it into a great trip. So I asked myself, *What's in Chicago?* I thought about trying to get on a local TV show to talk about my new book.

I thought about meeting with some people to arrange future speaking events on the inspirational topics that I am passionate about. Then, out of the blue, it hit me—*Oprah* is in Chicago!

I decided I was going to go and meet someone at HARPO Studios about my new book! Oprah had just done a couple of shows on the blockbuster hit DVD and book, *The Secret*, and *my* new book took *The Secret* to the next level. How perfect!

I was now standing in front of an amazing open door (that ironically was always there but had never noticed before). I was so excited! The excitement didn't last long though. I began to think about how hard it would be to actually meet with someone at HARPO. I started to doubt myself and my book. I thought that my efforts would just be a waste of time.

Shoot! I'm staring at that closed door again! I thought to myself. *Shift your thoughts about the situation, Sonia! Shift your thoughts!* So, I quickly did. I began surfing the Internet to find out who to contact at HARPO and *how* to contact them. It was no easy feat. In fact, it was nearly impossible to contact anyone specific there. I didn't want to contact them via the Oprah Website because I knew my message would be lost among the millions of e-mails they receive every day.

So I surfed, and surfed, and then surfed some more (for hours and hours), until I hit the jackpot. I found a list of all the producers at the *Oprah Show* and at *Oprah and Friends Radio*. I didn't know how old the list was, or if those people still worked there, but I thought I would give it a try anyway. One problem, though: I had a list of their names but not their contact information or e-mail addresses.

That stopped me for a few minutes, but there was no way I was going to give up. So I decided to try to guess their e-mail addresses! I tried every possible e-mail combination I could think of. They kept bouncing back to me. I felt a little discouraged, but not defeated. I continued. More than three hours had passed at this point, and I was beginning to go cross-eyed from staring at the computer, but I continued, until lo and behold—one e-mail didn't bounce back! Ecstatic, I thought to myself, *Oh my God, I broke the Oprah e-mail code!*

I immediately began to e-mail every single person on that list (there were at least 40). I sent each one of them a personalized e-mail about how I just wrote an amazing new book titled *Mastering the Law of Attraction*, and that I was going to be in Chicago for a few days, and then asked if I could meet with him or her in person.

Once that was done (at this point it was 3 a.m.), I went to bed. When I woke up later that morning, I ran to my computer and quickly looked to see if anyone responded. One person had. The message was short and sweet: "I can meet with you at 2 p.m. on Thursday." It was signed by a senior producer of Oprah and Friends Radio!

I almost fell off my chair. I was actually going to HARPO Studios to meet with a producer about my book! I couldn't believe it!

The Meeting That Changed My Life

I arrived that Thursday at HARPO Studios at 2 p.m. sharp. I couldn't believe I was really there. The entire experience was surreal. I was given a HARPO Studios visitors badge and asked to take a seat in the lobby. I was nervous and excited. Within minutes, a handsome, casually dressed man introduced himself as John St. Augustine and took me to his office.

The first question he asked me was, "So, Sonia, what brings you to Chicago?"

"I'm speaking at a health-club industry conference," I answered.

"Really? You work in the health-club industry?" he asked.

"I used to," I replied.

"You know, I used to be a personal trainer," he said.

We had something in common. We quickly hit it off. I felt as though I was speaking to an old friend. Our meeting was scheduled for 20 minutes, but the next thing I knew, an hour and a half had gone by. I found out that John produced *The Dr. Oz Show* and *The Jean Chaztky Show*, and was an accomplished talk radio host as well as being a best-selling author.

He loved my self-published book. He believed that the book was going to be a huge success; however, he felt that I needed a publisher for that to happen. For a brief moment I felt deflated. I knew what a difficult task it was going to be, as a first-time author, to get a publishing company to publish my book. The statistics were staggering and completely not in my favor.

Before I could even reply, he said, "Let me make a phone call for you."

He phoned the company that published his book *Living an Uncommon Life* and referred me to them. Within a few weeks, I had signed a contract with Hampton Roads Publishing to publish my book, now called *The Law of Attraction Plain and Simple*. It became a #1 best-seller and is currently sold all over North America, as well as in many other countries and in many different languages around the world.

To add icing to the cake, a few days later, John even arranged to have me as a guest on *Oprah and Friends Radio With Bob Green* (Oprah's personal trainer). The topic was "a behind-the-scenes look at the health-club industry." So, as it turned out, the reason I didn't want to go to Chicago was what actually got me a radio interview.

Think about it: If I had not chosen to step away from that closed door, I would have traveled to Chicago dragging my feet all the way there, presented my marketing presentation with a chip on my shoulder, and then returned home thinking that I had wasted three days of my life. Instead, I chose to focus on the open doors around me and my trip to Chicago turned out to be the best trip I have ever taken—just as I had intended! In fact, that trip to Chicago turned out to be a major turning point in my life and my career.

Tip

Think about all the areas/situations in your life you are unhappy about, complain about, and wish were different. Write them down. You are staring at a closed door in each of those areas. It is time to step away from those closed doors. It is time to shift your thoughts and focus on the positive side of every situation. Next to each statement, answer the following questions:

How can I view this situation differently and in a positive way?

What do I really want? (Thus removing the focus from what you don't want.)

What opportunities are there around me right now that will help me achieve what I really want in life?

Write your answers down and then create a statement of intention that describes what you want to achieve. By doing this, you have shifted your thoughts about the situation and are focusing on what you *want* to achieve (not on what you *don't* want). This shift in your thought process will allow you to become aware of the many opportunities all around you. You will be shocked at how many are right in front of you. You'll wonder how you ever missed them.

Then take action on the opportunities that have been presented to you!

Chapter 4:
Connect to Your
Higher Self

At the center of your being you have the answer;
You know who you are, and you know what you want.

—Lao Tzu

#12: Be Good to Yourself

Sometimes when we feel as though everything is falling apart all around us, we lose ourselves. Thinking straight is difficult to do, decisions are difficult to make, and solutions are difficult to find. But it is a time when your actions and decisions are critical to your future.

Often when a crisis occurs and we are thrown into a situation that is highly stressful in nature, our bodies react accordingly, and it can have quite a detrimental effect on our mental and physical health—depression, hair loss, heart disease, panic attacks, ulcers, and so many other health issues can arise. It is paramount to keep yourself in optimal mental and physical shape during difficult times. Take the time each day to be good to yourself.

Keep your mind fresh and your body healthy. Don't take this advice lightly! It could, in fact, be your saving grace. It is easy to let ourselves go when challenging times arise, but we need to be healthy mentally, physically, and emotionally in order to navigate through this journey. Having a fuzzy mind or a stressed body is not going to help you in your situation; in fact, it may worsen or prolong it.

Put yourself first and take time each day to take care of you. This may sound a little selfish, but the truth is, when you put yourself first you are equally putting everyone else first too. You see, when you take care of yourself, your stress levels are lowered, your mind is in a state of inner peace, and your tolerance levels are higher, so your relationships will benefit from it. The positive energy emanating from you will surely affect the people around you in a good way.

Of course, the opposite is also true: If you don't take care of yourself and instead are stressed, short-tempered, and mad at the world, you are emanating negative energy, which is not a pleasant or healthy environment for anyone to be around.

The following are nine key ways to be good to yourself that will assist you in gaining mental clarity, keeping your body healthy and your stress levels in check, and awakening your inner self. Each one of these is vital in helping you move forward and bounce back higher than ever.

    1. **Exercise.** Exercise in general is important to your health and well-being, but when tough times hit, it is absolutely crucial that you maintain a fitness regimen. The benefits of exercise are numerous.

In fact, exercise stimulates the release of endorphins, which elevates your mood and makes you feel good. Some other important benefits include:

❋ Reduction in stress levels

❋ Increased energy

❋ Illness prevention

❋ Increased self-esteem

❋ Improved mental clarity

You don't have to spend hours in the gym seven days a week to experience the benefits of exercise. Even if you simply exercise for 30 minutes three to four times a week, you will experience the benefits. There are many activities you can do that are beneficial to your physical and mental health, like yoga, swimming, walking, tennis, volleyball, hiking, and group exercise classes. Make sure you choose activities that you enjoy, or it will be difficult to stick with it.

2. **Meditate.** The benefits of meditation are endless. It is a phenomenal way to balance your emotional, physical, and mental state. Meditation not only reduces stress and puts you in a more peaceful state, but it has also been found to increase creativity, happiness, and overall health and well-being while decreasing depression, anxiety, and irritability. All you need to do is dedicate a few minutes each day to this practice.

3. **Take a time out.** When you get to a point at which you are overstressed and overwhelmed and feel as though you are ready to break, you need to take a time out.

Sometimes when you are too close to a difficult situation everything becomes a blur. All the obstacles and problems seem like huge mountains in front of you. By temporarily stepping away from everything, you will be able to see the situation in a different light.

Sometimes you just need to get out of the situation to clear your head. So stop and physically remove yourself from the situation in order to achieve the required clarity. Going away for a day or two would be ideal. That would mean going away alone—not with your children, spouse, friends, or family. You are going away to get clear, to reflect, and to bring some new perspective to your situation. It will be like standing at the top of the Empire State Building and looking down—the city below is your life. You will be able to view it from a different angle and gain clarity.

Do what it takes to make this time-out happen. If you absolutely cannot get away, then at least take several hours for yourself and do something you love, such as going to a museum, seeing a movie, getting a new haircut, or maybe going to the spa for a massage.

4. **Connect with nature.** People often feel a calming energy when communing with Mother Nature. Take regular walks in the woods, on the beach, or in a park. Notice the birds flying above, the trees swaying in the wind, and the clouds gliding ever so slowly in the sky. Experience and bask in all of nature's beauty.

5. **Laugh.** Numerous studies have been done on the healing effects of laughter, which include reducing pain, boosting the immune system, and overall making people feel happier. Laughter provides a physical and emotional release.

   You may not feel like laughing right now, but purposefully putting yourself in situations that are uplifting will help elevate your mood, clear your mind (while keeping your mind off of your current situation), and reduce your stress levels. You can watch a funny movie or TV show, be around fun friends, go see a stand-up comic show, or maybe read a funny article.

6. **Journal.** I am a huge fan of journaling. Writing down all your thoughts is a great way to release all the chaotic and foggy thinking going on in your mind. It's like having a conversation with yourself. What's amazing is that once you put your thoughts on paper, one of two things will happen: Either you (1) release all that negativity from your mind and experience mental clarity and focus, or (2) all of a sudden you come up with some incredible solutions to your situation. Sometimes you experience both! Journaling also helps you realize and become aware of what your true thinking patterns are so you can choose to consciously shift them if necessary.

7. **Take a deep breath.** I know this may sound somewhat trivial and maybe even ridiculous, but breathing is much more important than you may realize. Do you breathe deep and slow, or do you breathe

shallow and constricted? With all the daily stressors in our lives, most people breathe shallow and constricted. This type of breathing is not conducive to our health or well-being. Deep, slow breathing helps you feel relaxed and energized, decreases stress, and even improves heart function. Each day, take a "breathing break." Take the time to become aware of how you are breathing and consciously take deep, slow breaths. When you find yourself getting stressed, overwhelmed, or angry, stop and take a long deep breathe. You'll be amazed at how this will positively shift your state at that moment.

8. **Eat healthy.** Nutrition is very important during difficult times. This is not the time to eat fatty foods, sweets, and other foods that are not healthy for you. What you eat affects how you feel and how you think. It affects your energy level, your mental clarity, and even your ability to handle stress. It is essential to stick to a healthy and clean diet.

Often during difficult times, people use food as a crutch to manage stress. Many people eat lots of sugar, chocolate, chips, and other junk food as a temporary fix to feel better. But of course, it is only temporary, and it isn't good for you at all.

Become aware of what you are eating. Sometimes we eat without even thinking, which usually results in choosing foods that are bad for us. Plan your meals ahead of time, so you won't get side-tracked and seduced by that 99-cent burger that may be calling your name. Limit the amount of refined sugars, fats, and highly processed foods you consume. Stay away from candy, chocolate, chips, and packaged foods; instead, choose healthier and natural alternatives. It is also a good idea to choose organic versions of food items in order to avoid adding hormones or chemicals to your diet.

9. **Be in a positive environment.** Part of being good to yourself is ensuring that you expose your mind to positive stimuli. What this means is that you stay away from negative energy, which includes avoiding toxic people, negative media, and even managing your physical environment. It is difficult enough to maintain a positive state of mind when challenging life events are thrown our way, but it is even more difficult when we are also exposing ourselves to nonstop negativity, morning, noon, and night.

   We are actually bombarded with negativity all the time. Think about it: The news is constantly informing us of all the negative events in our neighborhoods and around the world. A lot of the music we listen to is filled with negative messages. At work, so many people are constantly complaining and gossiping. When we speak to our friends and family members they tell us about all the negative events happening in their lives (and others' lives).

   It isn't always easy to remove yourself from all this toxicity, but it is essential that you do your best to reduce it as much as possible. For instance, you can choose not to watch the news and instead watch a comedy, or perhaps pick up a book and read. Instead of listening to the radio, listen to your favorite CD that makes you feel good. Instead of actively participating and engaging in negative conversations at work, choose to change the subject to something uplifting and positive, or simply choose to refrain from participating in such conversations. When dealing with friends and family members, do your best to spend time with the people that uplift you the most (remember your circle of light). At times, you may find yourself stuck with someone who is being negative and draining your energy; when this happens, imagine yourself surrounded by an invisible shield of light. Say a prayer in your mind and set an intention such as, "May all negative energy be blocked by this shield, and only allow positive, loving energy through." You'll be amazed at the way this simple intention can make a huge difference in how you feel.

Maintaining a positive physical environment is important too—it is difficult to think clearly and feel good when you are surrounded by clutter and messiness. It can dramatically affect your state of mind, so clean up your environment. This means you must clean and organize your home, your work environment, and even your car! Remember that your direct physical environment can affect how you think as well as how you feel.

Tip

Honor your space both physically and mentally. Take time each and every day for yourself. This is YOU time. Whether it is in the morning before everyone else wakes up, at lunch time, or before you go to bed, doesn't matter. Schedule it if you have to—this appointment with "you" is just as important as any other meeting or appointment in your schedule, if not more so. This time for self-care is crucial to maintaining your sanity and your sense of calmness, and will help you get through a difficult time more quickly and with greater ease.

Also, make a conscious effort each day to ensure you maintain a positive environment. Set an intention each morning upon rising that you will surround yourself with positive people, positive music, positive media, and a clean and uncluttered environment. Doing so will help shift your energy and allow positive people, things, and situations to flow into your life.

#13: Listen to the Whispers

We are sent messages of light from a higher source all the time. These are important messages. Pay attention to them.

We often unwittingly choose to ignore these messages or are completely oblivious to them. They first arrive as soft whispers telling us that something is wrong, that we should do something, or that we need to let go of someone. Sometimes these messages are too painful to listen to, so we cast them aside—but that doesn't make them go away. Actually, the whispers get louder and louder, until you finally listen. Often, we have reached rock bottom by that point.

These whispers often present themselves as what we call "red flags." I guess you can say that I heard a whisper when I had that Wal-Mart conversation (mentioned in the Introduction). The message being sent was, "Beware. Investigate further. There is something seriously wrong here." I chose to ignore it. Looking back, I see that there were so many more messages and whispers sent my way. I chose to ignore each and every one of them. I wish I hadn't.

Pay attention to those quiet messages. They are being sent for a reason.

Tap Into Your Intuition

When we are looking for solutions to a problem, or need help figuring out what step to take next, we often go to the people around us to help give us the answers. Although it is fine to gain other people's perspective and advice, the truth is, they are not you. They have not walked in your shoes. They do not know what your heart truly desires and what makes your heart sing. They only know what they would do if *they* were in that situation, based on their own limiting beliefs and experiences through time. At times, this is a good thing because it helps you view the situation from a different angle and perhaps offers you some solutions you haven't thought of before; however, it can also cause more confusion, making your navigation to safety, happiness, and peace even more difficult.

You have all the answers you need. You simply need to gain mental clarity and get your mind into a quiet, peaceful state. Once you've done that, you ask for the answers.

This is tapping into your intuition. When you are mentally clear and your mind is in a peaceful state, the answers are there. Often, however, we don't trust our intuition, we get confused, or we are not happy with the answers we receive. So we ignore them.

If you are stressed out, angry, and frustrated, it will be difficult to access the right answers. In fact, decisions made during those mental states are highly toxic, and are coming from faulty thinking. This is not the time to make a decision or ask for answers; you may just end up making a bad situation worse.

You must get yourself into a clear, peaceful state of mind in order to get the answers you need to get you to the results for your highest good. Practicing the nine key ways to be good to yourself detailed earlier is instrumental in helping you tap into your intuition.

Always remember one very important thing: You already have all the answers. You simply need to connect to your higher self to gain access to them.

> ### Tip
>
> A great way to access the voice within is to meditate with intention. To do this, begin by sitting still and closing your eyes. Then set the intention of answering a particular question. Once you are clear with that, begin meditating. Don't force the answer to come; don't even think about it—simply quiet your mind and meditate. Once you are done meditating, lie down and close your eyes. Then ask the question again. See what answers come to you.

#14: Just "Be"

A quick and easy way to feel better instantly is to simply be present *in the present*. Just "be."

We spend a lot of our time worrying and thinking about the past or the future, and rarely focus on the present. The truth is, the past doesn't exist anymore. It is history. The only place the past exists is in our minds—in our memories, in our thoughts. But we tend to live our lives as if the past is still happening. The same goes for the future. We worry and stress about the future as if it is already happening. The most fascinating part is that we incessantly worry about the future, yet when the future arrives; it almost *never* turns out as badly as we had envisioned it.

As Winston Churchill once said: "When I look back on all these worries, I remember the story of the old man who said on his deathbed that he had had a lot of trouble in his life, most of which had never happened."

The next time your mind is overloaded with worry and uncertainty, stop and remind yourself that the present is all there is. This moment is all there is. There is no past. There is no future.

Our minds have a tendency to live in the past (focusing on something that has already happened) or in the future (focusing on something you anticipate *may* happen)—not in the present. By becoming present *in the present*, you are allowing yourself to simply appreciate your life right at that very moment. Just "be." Simply bask in the beauty of *the present* moment and watch your worries melt away.

I remember when I was at the peak of my difficult journey, this concept of just "being" and surrendering to the present moment helped me flow through the situation with greater ease. A perfect example of this is what I now call my "backyard experience."

My Backyard Experience

I feel exhausted. I haven't had a good night's sleep in such a long time. I have slept one too many times on that leather sofa. My neck is sore, my mind is a blur, and my back is throbbing with pain. These are all signs of severe stress. I know that.

I haven't seen the light at the end of the tunnel yet. Everything is pitch black. I am not sure what to do, what is going to happen, or how I am going to get out of this mess. The burden of showing a positive attitude for everyone involved, including my friends and family members, has consumed me completely.

Who am I? Who is this person? What happened to the old Sonia? My carefree days of being adventurous, taking risks, and living a happy-go-lucky, joyous life are now a dim memory. It feels as though those days are never to be again.

After spending hours in my home office replying to hundreds of e-mails, I knew I was just going through the motions. It was as though someone else had taken over my body and mind and did the work for me. I decided to take a break and just sit and reflect in my big backyard.

I brought a nice, tall, cold glass of lemonade to sip on and my little dog, Billie, with me. He is a 1-year-old Black Labrador mix whose name should really have been "Serenity"—his demeanor and presence project peace and happiness all the time.

I lay there enjoying the warmth of the July sun on my pale skin. The heat was comforting. Billie lay peacefully right next to me on the grass as I sipped on my cold, refreshing drink. I noted and began appreciating my surroundings—the beautiful aging trees, the birds flying around and chirping. I could hear children playing and giggling nearby. The sound of a woodpecker echoed loudly.

It wasn't long before *the thoughts* began taking over my fragile mind. *What am I going to do? How am I going to get out of this mess? Why is this happening? I need to get out of this situation. I need to get out of this relationship. I don't even know who he is anymore. I can't get out. He won't survive if I leave. How can I leave someone who is hitting rock bottom? What kind of person would do that? We are going to lose this beautiful house, this beautiful backyard. Where are we going to live?*

This grim conversation with myself went on for a long while. Unfortunately, no answers came to light. I was just feeling confusion, stress, and emotional pain. I suddenly became present to my dog licking my hand draped over the side of the chair. I smiled. *What a sweet, sweet dog.* I took a deep breath in, and slowly exhaled. *What am I doing?* I asked myself. *Why am I torturing myself this way? Here I am sitting in my backyard, in the middle of the week (while the world is out working), sipping on a cold lemonade, basking in the warm sunlight, as my little pooch is affectionately licking my hand trying to gain my attention.*

"Just be, Sonia, just be," whispered my inner voice. "Enjoy the present moment, for that is all we have. The past is gone and the future is yet to come."

Hmmm, "just be," I thought to myself.

My life and the world around me seemed to transform in front of my eyes. *Wow, look at how beautiful everything is. I am so grateful for all that I have right now, right this second.* I felt a sense of peace flow through my body.

Problems? What problems? I don't have any problems.

Tip

Set aside time each day to connect with nature and your surroundings. Take a long walk, go to the beach, go to the park, or sit in your own backyard. Observe everything around you—the bird flying up above, the squirrel scurrying up the tree, the children playing, the formation of the clouds in the sky, the sound of the water sprinklers, and so on.

Doing this each day will exercise your "be present" muscle. At first, you will notice your mind wandering, but with practice, it will get easier and easier. Eventually, you will have the power to gain access to this peaceful state of *just being* anytime, anywhere, and no matter what the circumstances.

Chapter 5:
Let Love Lead

If you judge people, you have no time to love them.
—Mother Theresa

#15: Forgive Yourself and Others

When we have been wronged, our first defense is to feel resentment and anger for the offending person or situation. This is our way of protecting our heart from feeling the true pain it is feeling. What we don't realize is that holding this resentment and anger will only augment and prolong the pain, making moving forward and past what has happened more difficult.

We often believe that holding on to these negative feelings lets us get back at that offending person, when in fact we are not getting back at anyone but ourselves, and are also giving that person control over our emotions.

Keep in mind, as I mentioned earlier in this book, that what you are currently feeling does not come from the external circumstances in your life, but your thoughts about those circumstances. No one can *make* you feel angry or resentful. You hear people say all the time, "She made me so angry!" In reality, that isn't correct. She chose to do or say something to you and you chose to have a certain thought about it, which led to you feeling angry and resentful.

We have a lot more control over how we feel than we think we do, and once we realize that, life becomes a more peaceful and joyful experience. And when you live life in this positive state, you will also attract more positive experiences into your life—an added bonus.

The act of forgiveness is important in order to move forward in your life. If you want to bounce back quickly and higher than you ever thought possible, it is necessary that you forgive anyone involved in (or was part of) what happened in your situation.

Let it go, send love their way (because chances are they really need it), and move forward. One way of looking at it is like this: Hurt people hurt people. People don't just go out and say and do mean and hurtful things just for the sake of being mean. There are reasons behind the behavior that we most likely will never know or understand. Most likely, it has absolutely nothing to do with us.

At times the person we need to forgive is ourselves. Sometimes we do or say things we are not proud of, and we feel badly about it. We can often be our own worst enemy. This needs to stop immediately. Loving yourself is of prime importance when moving forward and bouncing back from a challenging situation. Each moment of every day is an opportunity to start fresh. Remember, the past is history; it's gone; you can't change it, so let it go. Keeping it alive through your thoughts or punishing yourself for something you cannot go back and change is futile and self-defeating. It helps no one.

The act of forgiving can have such healing effects that it can not only shift how you feel about the person or people involved, but it also shifts something in you, and ultimately this release and newfound inner peace and freedom will change your situation and your life.

Forgiving someone is not easy. It is probably one of the most difficult things you can do. It is necessary, however, in order for you to move forward.

Look for the Silver Lining

If you are having difficulty forgiving someone, you can first begin by looking for the silver lining to whatever happened. Like the old adage states, "every cloud has a silver lining." It may not be easy to find. It may take a while to find it. But *every* situation has a silver lining.

A while ago, I had the pleasure of having a beautiful and inspiring 18-year-old attend one of my Live Life Out Loud Miracle Weekend workshops. Samantha was special, and a true inspiration to everyone in the room. Samantha was no *regular* teenager. When I arrived that morning, she was standing outside of the room where the workshop was about to begin. As soon as I saw her, I immediately felt drawn to her and gave her the biggest hug. The love and positive energy she exuded was off the charts.

A year before, Samantha was diagnosed with osteosarcoma, a type of bone cancer. She had undergone surgery and many rounds of chemotherapy. She had, in fact, just had chemotherapy treatment the day before the workshop. Samantha had been in and out of hospitals undergoing aggressive treatment for more than a year—not exactly the life of a typical teenager.

On a few occasions during the workshop she had to leave the room because she was feeling so sick and nauseous, a side-effect of the chemotherapy. Each time she returned to the room, although appearing a little weak, she always had a big smile on her face. I was amazed at how positive and happy she was. You couldn't help but be happy and feel good around her. I was happy to have her sit in the front row.

What amazed me the most was when she courageously stood up in front of everyone and read her "forgiveness" letter. Everyone in the workshop was required to write about a story from their past that had negatively affected them. The purpose of the exercise was to experience the freedom one feels when forgiving someone. Part of the exercise was finding the silver lining in the situation, along with the lesson learned and the growth experienced. They were then asked to write a letter forgiving that person.

I asked if anyone wanted to share their letter with the group, and Samantha offered to read hers. Her forgiveness letter was to a doctor at her hospital. Her usual doctor was on vacation, and this doctor was covering for him.

Dear Dr. R.,

I am writing this letter to you as I have been holding a lot of resentment and anger toward you since our last meeting. Last August I had an appointment to see you and what you told me that day devastated me. You said that by Christmas my lungs would be in bad shape and that I would be suffering severely from the side effects from this. You said that I should sit down with my parents and get all my "affairs in order." What you said next is what really hurt me the most. You said, "Don't sit around waiting for a miracle."

What you said really had a negative impact on me. I was devastated and angry. Very angry. You tried to take away my hope and dreams.

Those devastating words prompted my two sets of parents (my mom, dad, stepmom, and stepdad) and me to go on a trip to New York City a week later. We stayed at the Ritz Carlton Hotel and then took a four-day cruise from NYC to New Brunswick. It was an amazing trip and a much-needed one for all. A trip we would not have taken had you not said what you said. It helped us to stand back up tall and be completely full of hope and faith—gifts that no one has the right to take away.

Now, here we are many months later and I am grateful for that conversation and want to thank you for saying those words. Your words made me realize the unwavering strength that I have to fight and conquer this disease. I know that with faith, continuous love, and the power of positive thinking, it will happen. I have also realized that I want to be an inspiration to others.

Today, I am still here, and I believe every day to be a gift from God, and now every day for me is a miracle.

Yours truly,
Samantha

As you can see, even in Samantha's difficult situation she was able to change her perception and shift her feelings by finding a silver lining to her doctor's words. His words upset her—understandably so—but once she was able to find the silver lining around them she was able to release her anger toward the doctor, shift her perspective on her situation, and find it in her heart to forgive and even thank him for saying what he said. Now *that* is powerful.

We truly do hold the key to our own happiness. Forgiving others and ourselves is a key step to moving forward toward living a life filled with peace, love, and happiness.

Tip

Forgiving someone is not always easy. This exercise will help you release negative feelings and set you free.

1. Close your eyes and think of the hurtful experience that occurred. Feel the emotions that come up.

2. Become aware of your thoughts. Realize and acknowledge that your

emotions are arising from your thoughts about what happened. Write down these thoughts.

3. Close your eyes again. Now think of the lessons you've learned and how much you have grown because of what happened, and look for the silver lining. Write it down. Now that you have become present to the lessons you have learned and realized that there *was* a silver lining to that situation, you can now shift your thoughts about what happened.

4. Write a letter to the person you wish to forgive and thank him or her. Explain to the person all the lessons you've learned, how you have grown, and that you now see it was a blessing in disguise. Then, forgive the person.

This exercise can be done to forgive people who have already passed away as well. You don't have to give the person the letter for the act of forgiveness to occur. The act of forgiveness is something very personal to you, and it is done to set you free.

#16: Always Come From a Place of Love

Nothing is ever as we think it is. We have only our interpretation and perception of "what is." Based on this we decide how to react to a situation or to a person. If you want to remain in a peaceful state in any situation, don't jump to conclusions, overanalyze what is "really" going on, or interpret what someone "really" meant. Don't judge it at all. Simply "be," and send love their way.

Practicing unconditional love is a beautiful thing. It isn't always easy to do and certainly takes practice, but it truly is an incredible way to remain in peace in any circumstance. It also shifts the energy not only in you, but also in the people around you. Let's face it, loving someone feels a lot better than being angry at someone. We don't know why people do what they do (and often they don't even know themselves); we have not walked in their shoes, and we don't know what is going on inside of them. So when we react to a person in a negative way, we are doing so without all the facts and without understanding what is really going on. Perhaps it is best, then, to not react to it at all.

Whenever I find myself in a situation in which I know I am getting agitated or upset, the first thing I say over and over in my mind before responding is, "Come from a place of love. Come from a place of love. Come from a place of love." And *then* I respond. This small phrase has defused many arguments for me. You'll be amazed at how quickly you are able to shift your feelings and your situation when you come from this beautiful place.

Marci Shimoff, my friend and *New York Times* best-selling author of many books, including *Happy for No Reason*, is an expert in achieving unconditional love. In her latest book, *Love for No Reason*, she outlines exactly what it takes to live a life of unconditional love. She has offered her words of wisdom to this book and shares some tips that will help you live in a state of unconditional love all the time—even during difficult times.

THE TOP 10 TIPS FOR LIVING IN LOVE DURING CHALLENGING TIMES— MARCI SHIMOFF

What if you could live in a state of unconditional love all the time, even when going through a life crisis? You can. What's more, being in that loving state can actually dramatically shift your challenging situation. You see, when you're open-hearted and loving, you magnetize those qualities to yourself—you attract the good because you're radiating the good.

In my book *Love for No Reason*, I interviewed more than 150 people I call "Love Luminaries," including scientists, psychologists, spiritual teachers, and people whose lives were rich in the qualities of the heart. These people weren't just experiencing a Hollywood or Hallmark kind of love, but love as a state of being; the kind of love that is limitless and doesn't ask to be returned. The state I call "Love for No Reason."

What I found is that although the Love Luminaries come from all walks of life and have diverse personalities, they share certain qualities that we can all develop to experience more unconditional love.

Here are 10 tips from my book *Love for No Reason* that will help you achieve this magical state of unconditional love even during trying times.

1. Anchor yourself in safety. Feeling stressed, unsupported, or fearful essentially takes love offline. It's impossible to activate the physiology of unconditional love when you're experiencing stress and your body is in fight-or-flight. To quickly switch out of stress mode, take a few deep breaths and consciously relax your pelvic floor, located at the base of your body. This kick-starts your parasympathetic system and sets the stage for what mind/body health expert Dr. Eva Selhub calls your body's "love response."

2. Sense your support. Einstein once said that the most important decision you can make is whether to believe you live in a friendly universe—one that is always supporting you. When you're facing a challenge in life, sense the support of this friendly universe by looking for ways the situation is ultimately serving you. Ask yourself, *Is this for my enjoyment, growth, or both?* This helps you avoid generating the biochemistry of anger and sadness and keeps your love flowing.

3. Feel your feelings. What I discovered from my research is that stifling your emotions is equally as damaging to your capacity to experience love as expressing them excessively. Luckily, there's a third option: *feeling* your feelings. Practice experiencing your feelings directly and completely by observing them as they move through your mind and body—and then letting them go.

4. Practice self-compassion. Try a simple self-love technique that brings you into your heart and reminds you to treat yourself with care. Throughout the day, ask yourself, *What's the most loving thing I can do for myself right now?* or *What's the most loving way I can be with myself right now?* Then pay attention to the answer and actually *do* whatever it is. When you love and take care of yourself, you'll find it inevitably serves everyone.

5. Unleash the power of forgiveness. If you're holding on to any resentments or grudges—past or present—they're blocking your ability to love. Use the ancient Hawaiian kahuna technique of Ho'oponopono to release and forgive. The technique consists of sitting quietly and mentally repeating, "I'm sorry. Please forgive me. Thank you. I love you," over and over. Based on the principle of taking total responsibility for everything that happens to you, Ho'oponopono allows you to bring the vibration of pure forgiveness into any situation.

6. Let love in. Receiving from others is an act of love and connection that opens your heart and benefits your body too. Research shows that when you receive gifts, your levels of serotonin (the neurotransmitter of well-being and happiness) rise just as much as when you give gifts. The next time someone offers you a gift, whether in the form of a present, a compliment, or some assistance, graciously receive it. Smile and say thank you, while consciously feeling appreciation in your heart.

7. Live with a grateful heart. Start your own gratitude practice by consciously registering and savoring all that you're receiving right now. Gratitude is the fast track to love. List five things you are grateful for at the end of each day. Doing so turned my life around, and it will do the same for you.

8. Speak the language of love. When we speak directly from the place of unconditional love inside us, we touch that same love in the people we're speaking to. To amp up the wattage of your love-body and have the most positive influence on the world around you, use words that transmit frequencies of love, not fear.

9. Listen for the subtitles. During a conversation, wouldn't it be nice to be able to read subtitles that spelled out what the other person really meant? If you only listen to the words spoken, rather than the underlying intention, you can end up feeling blamed or attacked. But when you hear from your heart, your body's fear system shuts off and you stop seeing the other person as an enemy. Instead, you see the person's humanity and how alike the two of you are, cultivating more compassion and love. Create a safe space for others to communicate with you by being sensitive to the unspoken feelings and needs that underlie people's words.

10. Plug in to a larger heart. Love thrives when we feel at peace inside. Recharge your spiritual batteries by investing time each day in silence, meditation, or prayer. Tapping into this inner wellspring of spirit will connect you to the energy of unconditional love and boost your capacity to experience Love for No Reason to infinite levels.

Making these 10 simple but powerful tips part of your daily life will help you experience this wonderful state of unconditional love more and more often. When your heart is open, both your internal and external worlds shift for the better. Even the people around you are affected in a beautiful and magical way.

Unconditional love is truly the one thing that changes everything.

> ### Tip
>
> The next time you find yourself becoming agitated or upset with someone, before you respond, stop. Think to yourself, *How can I come from a place of love in this situation right at this moment?* Instead of reacting in a negative manner, consciously send the person love. There is a really good chance he or she needs it.

#17: Be Grateful for All That Is and All That Will Be

Have an attitude of gratitude. I'm sure you've heard this statement before. It is a powerful one that can shift how you feel in a split second. We all have a lot to be grateful for in our lives (even when going through challenging times). Taking the time to think about all the great things we do have in our lives gives us the opportunity to focus on the good, and helps put everything in perspective. Sometimes we get so caught up with the small details of our situation that we forget the bigger picture and the incredibly wonderful life we really do have.

I remember a while back I was lying in bed in the dark getting ready to fall asleep. The devastating earthquake had just hit Haiti, and as I was saying a prayer for all the people who had been injured and killed, I began to think of the millions who had been displaced and were simply sleeping out in the streets. At that moment, I became present to the bed I was sleeping in. How warm it was, how soft it was, how comforting and comfortable it was. I began to think and feel how lucky I was to have a bed to sleep in.

Being grateful for all that is wonderful in your life is so important, and once you have mastered that, I'd like you to take it a step further.

Be grateful for all that *will* be. That is, be grateful now for what your life will be in the future. Get in the feeling of having moved forward, having successfully overcome your obstacles, and imagine how wonderful it will be living your *new* life. You don't have to wait for this to actually happen before being grateful for it. Visualize your new life. Feel and get in touch with what it will be like. This will not only elevate how you feel at that moment (knowing there is a bright light at the end of the tunnel), but the positive energy you will generate by doing this will also help you attract it into your life.

Tip

Take the time to write out everything you are grateful for in your life. Once you have done that, write a letter to yourself as if you are already in the future. Write out how grateful you are living your new life, after you have overcome your obstacles, and are now on the other side living in this bright new world. Be detailed in your description

> so you can truly feel and imagine what it is
> like to live that life. While doing this, look
> for the silver lining. How was that obstacle
> a blessing in disguise? Be creative; have
> fun with it. This scenario will be only one
> of many possible wonderful outcomes in
> your future. Don't judge it or spend hours
> trying to figure out the "right" outcome. It
> doesn't matter; just write. It will help you
> feel what it is like to reach the other side of
> this situation.

I'd like to close this chapter on forgiveness, love, and gratitude with Joann Brnjas's stirring tale of losing her daughter, Samantha (whom you might remember from the forgiveness letter earlier in the chapter), to cancer—and yet never losing her hope or faith.

Joann Brnjas

Just 22 months ago, my dearest Samantha died. Her head fell into in my left hand as she took her last breath. Her eyes were fixed and frozen on mine.

Sam was my youngest child—rather, *still is* my youngest child. At 17 she was diagnosed with osteosarcoma. Even after limb salvage surgery, the disease continued to ravage her body, showing no mercy. Bone cancer is incredibly painful, and Sam's disease was incredibly aggressive. She died seven weeks before her 19th birthday.

I was completely devastated. Today, I am still devastated.

We hoped for a much different ending to this traumatic invasion of Sam's body. During this journey with cancer, we talked about and dreamed of the future so many times. The day would come, we said, when Sam would look back upon this experience and tell her two, maybe even three children just how courageous and brave she was when she was just a young girl! And she would have the scars to prove it. Yes, Sam would recover, grow up to have a family of her own, and be able to share her story with many for years to come. One day we would put all this behind us and even share laughs over some of the crazy things we encountered during her illness.

But things didn't turn out the way we envisioned—an understatement of a fact I wish I had better words to express. But I am still here today, existing, breathing, carrying on with daily living, and also mending my heart, as many others are. I am slowly learning how to desire life, and am challenging myself to consider giving myself permission to enjoy it again—something I suspect any parent who loses a child might contend with.

Rewind to the Diagnosis

Ironically, less than a year earlier, I had attended a local fundraising luncheon for the disease. As I sat at my table, everyone shared their experience of a very close family member's brush with a cancerous death threat. When it was my turn, I felt so fortunate to say I was one of the lucky ones—no parents, grandparents, spouses, siblings (nor, heaven forbid, children) had been plagued with that darkness.

So when Sam was diagnosed with cancer, I was unprepared. It caught me completely off guard. *How on earth am I going to protect Samantha from this?* I wondered. I had no time to waste! I believed I needed to be one step ahead of Samantha so that I could provide support and help her to be prepared for whatever might come the next day, and every day thereafter. I felt that I needed an elaborate plan for every eventuality, but I also knew that I had to relinquish control to the grace of God.

Aim, Focus, Stay the Course

God's attention and participation was the prime target for me. I put faith and trust at the top of my pyramid, and I was truly thankful that Samantha held her own with a strong belief of faith. We didn't always understand the ways of divinity, but we also didn't know *what we didn't know* in our grounded living. We kept our aim focused on high.

We learned that hope is within your control. Friends, doctors, and Websites can give you facts, statistics, and calculated probabilities, but hope is yours to decide how much of it you have. It's a gift, and it's your right to have it, so use it. When the clouds covered up our target, we used hope to clear the path so we could stay on track.

We kept a stranglehold on hope right up to Sam's final day with us. I assure you, hope is not denial. There is a clear difference between the two. Denial is refusing to absorb the facts, whereas hope is purposefully choosing to stay in the game *despite* the facts. It's your life, your game, your call. As a very young adult, Sam learned that we are not in control of what our tomorrows bring, and we have to roll with what we cannot change. But we *could* control and manage our levels of hope and our disposition.

We learned what a beast anticipation can be. It plops into your life and can grow vigorously if left alone. Overwhelming anticipation can easily throw one off track. From the date of diagnosis, a seed of anticipation was immediately planted in our minds. Like Jack's beanstalk, this anticipation grew and grew. We needed an effective strategy to manage the growth of this anticipation with positive things. We dissolved the heavy anxiety with the countless ways of embracing the joys of life and loved ones. We allowed ourselves to use up our anxious energy by waiting for positive things to happen! It's far more fun to be anxiously waiting for an evening out with friends than your next round of chemo.

Aiming our targets high, having hope, and embracing life each and every day was how we got through the journey. We never for a second could imagine our lives without Sam. And so we didn't. Rather, we embraced every moment of the present. I can look back and be so very thankful for the absolutely wonderful moments that were spent enjoying life, like the endless giggling during overnight stays at the hospital; jumping and dancing on hotel beds to Mama Mia; running around to various places to obtain what it was that she felt like eating—only to discover she changed her mind; endless and ongoing planning! Weekends away, cruises, shopping trips and movie nights, and then critically assessing them after the fact. One of my favorites was watching family members scramble when Sam yelled "b-u-c-k-e-t!" She rarely missed. Also, I looked back at listening to Sam provide life advice to her friends, knowing that it came straight from her heart, and witnessing how she genuinely loved them all, as well as all her family members. Learning in a late-night soulful discussion that her fears of death were for those left behind. One of the most beautiful things was seeing and experiencing my child at the absolute optimum level of strength and courage, love and faith—she was so incredibly inspiring. We not only reached our target, but we surpassed it, all with God's grace.

The Strength Within

I believe there is a part of us that is able to provide comfort and assurance regardless of what is happening. It lifts you up and seems to know far more than we do. I think this character should be given more respect, more head and heart time. I think we need to get to know it better and protect it.

My very being has changed. I face the challenge of "you can do better" when it comes to all personal relationships. I have learned a very precious life lesson to truly embrace the current day and all that it presents to you. The thought of my other children, my grandchildren, and all my family members keeps me going. Each day is also a day closer to that miraculous day when I will be with Samantha again. However, thoughts of my family keep me grounded and wanting to enjoy every new day as it comes.

It may not have been meant to be, for Samantha to be healed from her cancerous attack, but, without question, Samantha was meant to be.

Chapter 6:
Give to Feel Good

For it is in giving that we receive.

—St. Francis of Assisi

#18: Step Outside of Yourself

Many people say that they would love to help others in need but can't because they have to get through their own personal crisis/situation first. *How can I give to others when I don't have much myself?* they wonder. Once they are taken care of, *then* they will help others.

Sorry, that's not how it works. When you step outside of yourself (and your situation) to help another in need, you will be amazed by what occurs. First, you feel good right away. Although it is wonderful to receive, giving to another person and making a difference in his or her life makes you feel good too!

I have been on many humanitarian trips around the world, and several people have made comments to me like, "Wow, that's really commendable of you, Sonia." What most people don't realize is that I get more out of giving than do the people on the receiving end. I can't tell you how good giving to another makes *me* feel. By simply stepping outside of yourself and helping others, you are putting aside your problems for a moment and gaining perspective on what is going on outside of your world. This alone can shift your mental state to a more positive one.

There are many different ways you can give. You can give money to a charitable organization, volunteer your time, shovel the driveway for an elderly neighbor, or buy a sandwich for a homeless person. Whatever it is, just do something outside of yourself that will help another person. Go out of your way to do it. Set the intention each day to do something good for another. You'll be amazed at how that will change the way you feel.

The Law of Giving and Receiving

What I find amazing is that when you go out of your way to give to another person, you will also receive great things in your life. This is what is called the Law of Giving and Receiving. You may not receive from the people you are helping, but you will receive good things from other people and in other ways. Pay attention to this law and notice how it works.

You need to get really great at both giving *and* receiving. I find that sometimes when you are in a difficult situation, you are in survival mode. When that happens, you can easily fall into the behavior of only focusing on the receiving part of this law by concentrating on what you can do for *yourself* to help *yourself*, and ways others can help *you*. There is nothing wrong with this thinking, per se, because you do need to take action and find solutions to help you overcome your situation, but there should be a balance. If you are *only* focusing on what you can get *from* people, then the flow of energy stops.

Of course, when you are giving, your intention behind the act is important too. You can't give with the sole purpose and expectation of receiving something in return. It doesn't work that way. It has to come from a pure place. Give because you want to give. Give because it is the right thing to do. You'll be amazed by what is returned to you when you give from that beautiful place.

Getting good at giving is important in shifting your situation and your life. It is also just as important to get really good at receiving. It is amazing how many people out there have trouble receiving! How often do you hear someone say, "Oh, you shouldn't have," or, "Why did you do that? You didn't have to do that," or, "Oh, no, I can't accept that"?

Please remember that when you are receiving a gift of any sort, whether it be an actual object or an act of kindness, the person who is giving to you is also getting something wonderful out of it—it makes him or her feel good to do it, so don't take that joy away. Receive it. Receive it with open arms, with gratitude and love. This will make both of you feel good. Don't feel guilty for receiving it or feel as though you have to give something back to that person. Simply receiving it graciously is a gift in return.

Cynthia Kersey's story is a perfect example of the way giving, especially during difficult times, can transform and shift your life. She is the *New York Times* best-selling author of *Unstoppable* and *Unstoppable Women*, and she has offered to share her very poignant story with you here.

GIVING CAN SAVE YOU DURING TRYING TIMES—CYNTHIA KERSEY

In December 1999, 21 months after my first book, *Unstoppable*, was published, my husband of 20 years and I separated. We had met in college and I fully intended to be married to him for the rest of my life. For those of you who have experienced this type of loss, you know how difficult and painful it can be.

My husband had intended to join my son and me for the holidays at my parents' house in Florida, but now my son and I would be going alone. The first few days at my parents' house were excruciating. I was in great pain and had momentarily lost my hope for a happy future. After a few days of feeling sorry for myself, I realized that I couldn't control what was happening. The only thing I could control was my response to my circumstances. In that moment, I vowed that the next Christmas, I would not be feeling sorry for myself at my parents' house. I would instead dedicate myself to doing something for someone else.

When I got home, I called my mentor and friend, Millard Fuller, the founder of Habitat for Humanity International (HFH), whom I had met when I interviewed him for my book. He told me that when you have a great pain in your life you need a greater purpose, and said that building a house for a family in need might be a great project for me. He had just returned from a trip to Nepal, one of the poorest nations in the world, and suggested I join the next house-building expedition there. Following Millard's advice, I asked myself the question, "How many houses do I need to build to offset this pain in my life?" When I got to 100, that number felt bigger than my pain.

I had never been to Nepal, I'd never raised money for a project such as this before, and I had no idea how I would pull it off, but having that purpose invigorated me—and, most importantly, it kept my mind off of myself and my "problems." Even though there were many times when I felt so depressed I didn't even want to get out of bed, I'd think about these Nepalese families who didn't have a decent place to sleep at night. That put my life back in perspective and I continued to move forward.

By December 2000, I had raised $200,000 and took a team of 20 people to Nepal, and we built the first three of the 100 houses in that project. One of the homes was for a single woman named Chandra who was supporting seven other family members, including her parents, brothers, and sisters. They had all been living in a small one-bedroom shack. Even though she consistently saved money every week from her job at a cookie factory, it would never have been enough to build a home without the help of HFH.

Even though we didn't speak the same language, Chandra and I connected. When it was time for us to leave, she began to cry and said, "Please don't ever forget me." I thought, *How could I forget you? You were the purpose that kept me going through the most difficult year of my life.*

That experience was truly one of the most transformational experiences in my life, and it was the first time I personally experienced the power of giving. Even more interesting, during that year, I made more money than I ever made in my life, even though that was not my primary intention.

I believe this story represents the essence of the Law of Giving and Receiving. You don't need to be experiencing pain or loss to feel the immense rewards of helping others. You also don't need to set out to build 100 homes. Start small. Start with helping to provide clean water for a child or a hot lunch for children who are going without. You can find out about all the different programs you can begin aiding today by going to *www.unstoppablefoundation.org.*

The scriptures say, "Give and it shall be given unto you." They don't say, "Wait until your life is working and then give," or "Wait until you feel you have something to give before you give." They simply say GIVE. You don't need to know how it will all work out; you only need to have faith that when you are committed, you will be supported. When you connect with a divine calling that is bigger than yourself, miracles await you.

As you can see from Cynthia Kersey's story, stepping outside of yourself when going through tough times is really important. Focusing on others will not only dramatically shift how you feel and shift your perspective on your situation, but you will also notice a lot of amazing things coming back to you. This remarkable shift in your thinking will ultimately transform the situation itself.

Tip

Each day, consciously do something kind for another person. Step outside of your everyday routine and do at least one nice thing for another person. It can be something big, such as depositing money into a friend's account who is going through some financial difficulties, or perhaps sponsoring a child in a developing country. Or it can be something small, such as letting the person behind you in line at the grocery store go ahead of you. Just do something kind, large or small. Of course, it has to be done with a pure, loving heart, with no strings attached and with no expectations of getting anything back in return. You'll be amazed what will come back to you. The Universe (or God, or whatever term you choose to use) works in mysterious ways.

Chapter 7:
Step Into Your Greatness

The journey of a thousand miles begins with a single step.
—Lao Tzu

#19: Within Every Crisis Lies a Golden Opportunity

I made a powerful statement after I had my meltdown. It was a declaration of sorts:

Something great is going to come out of this. I don't know what yet, but something amazing, huge, incredible will come out of it. Something so big; way bigger than me. I will make sure of it, because there is no way I am going through all THIS for nothing!

Little did I know at the time how those powerful words would set in motion events far beyond what I ever imagined was possible. That statement helped me step away from that closed door I was staring at and allowed me to instead look at the open doors around me. Those open

doors weren't immediately available to me, but I was looking. I knew they were there. I believed. I had faith that
something magnificent was going to be unveiled.

About two weeks after that meltdown, I found my
open door—I knew that my new calling was to help others
going through difficult times. I knew I needed to learn all
the lessons I could in order to grow from this experience. I
was eagerly searching for lessons.

Within every crisis lies a golden opportunity. Often,
people are completely oblivious to the opportunity that
has been handed to them, most likely because they are
intently focusing on the closed door. There is a huge opportunity waiting for you. You may not know what that is
yet, but just know it is there. With time it will be revealed
to you, if you so choose.

Tip

It is now time to sit yourself down, grab
a pen and pad, and begin creating your
own personal declaration. It doesn't have
to be the same as mine; choose words that
resonate for you. Words that feel powerful
and positive to you. It can be just a sen-
tence or two, or even more if you'd like.
There is no right or wrong way to create
this declaration. Post it in a visible place
where you can be reminded of it regularly.

#20: Live a Maverick Life

It is your time. It is your time to break free, move forward, and begin your *new* life. It's time to leave behind what was, take the lessons you have learned, and do something great with them. It's time to begin living the life you love and desire. Right now. Not tomorrow, not one day, not when the stars line up or when all your ducks are in order—right now. It's time to take action. Simply by making this decision, you will automatically be pointed and propelled in the direction that is intended for your higher good.

Remember these three words: Think. Step. Live.

Think outside the box. *Step* outside of the box. *Live* outside the box.

I believe that best describes a "maverick."

Be different.

If you want to live an extraordinary life, you have to step away from the crowd. You have to be prepared to walk your own path. At times, when you do this, people may not agree with what you are doing; they may laugh at or mock you, and they may very well think you're crazy. Get used to it. Don't allow others to rain on your parade. Stay focused and maintain your vision.

You will notice that many of the naysayers are people who are close to you, and often their opinions and advice are coming from a loving and well-intended place. Respect that. Send them love, acknowledge their concern, and thank them for sharing their thoughts and advice. Ultimately, however, you have to do what's best for you and your life, and this may be very different from what others around you think is best for you and your life. Of course, they are entitled to their opinions just as you are entitled to yours, but remember, this is *your* life.

One thing I learned a long time ago is that I cannot control how others feel, think, react, or behave. I used to live my life always trying to please others, and I would behave in ways that I knew would make others close to me happy even if it wasn't what I wanted to do and it didn't make *me* happy.

One day, I had had enough. One day it occurred to me that I actually had no real control over how others feel, think, react, or behave. I realized that as much as I tried to make others happy (many times at the expense of my own happiness), they never really behaved and reacted the way I expected and wanted them too anyway. It was all an illusion of control.

I began living a maverick life in my mid 20s. Up until then, I had followed the crowd and done what I was supposed to. I didn't stick out. I blended in beautifully. But once I finally blossomed and took control of my own life, I really began to live.

Living a maverick life is not always easy. Sometimes you have to really think differently than most do. Sometimes you have to make sacrifices. Sometimes you have to go against the grain, and at times it can be a lonely road. In the end, however, it is all worth it.

I remember one of the first times I really spread my wings and began flying on my own. I had been working for a tour operator in the customer relations department. I would spend eight hours a day, five days a week listening to people complain. Being in such a negative environment really took a toll on me. I was burnt out, tired, and miserable. I was ready for a change.

Having lived my entire life in the Great White North (Canada), I lived through brutal winters year after year. I had always had a dream to live and work down south at some tropical destination. I loved to daydream and visualize living this beautiful life by the beach, enjoying the hot sun in a very relaxed, laid-back environment. So I began investigating and researching what it would take to make this dream a reality. I found out that there was a job that would allow me to live and work in tropical destinations, working for tour operators. I would essentially be their representative at a vacation destination, handling any problems and offering destination information to the travelers.

I wanted that job.

There was just one problem: The job required that the representative speak Spanish. I didn't speak Spanish.

Although at first I was somewhat deflated, I didn't give up. I *really* wanted that job. I decided to go ahead and apply for the position anyway. I knew that they would be doing the interviews in September and the job wouldn't begin until December, so I figured I would have two to three months to learn the language. I remember getting the phone call, about two weeks later, inviting me to an interview for my dream job as if it was yesterday: The recruiter said, "We would like to interview you for the position of destination representative. Would you be available to come in on Tuesday at 2 p.m.?" I was so excited. My dream was about to come true! Then he said, "We will do the majority of the interview in English, but we have to also test your Spanish so we will be doing part of the interview in Spanish."

My heart sank. Game over. My dream was shattered.

I was completely caught off guard and I didn't know what to say. After a few seconds, these were the words that came out of my mouth: "Okay, that's great! I will see you on Tuesday at 2 p.m. Thank you for this opportunity!" and hung up the phone.

I sat there dumbfounded. I began to panic. *What did I just do? Why did I say yes to the interview? I can't go to that interview. They'll find out I don't speak Spanish! I will make a total fool of myself!* I wanted that job so badly though. So I began to think outside the box. *How can I make this dream of mine come true? How can I get this job?* A crazy thought entered my mind. I wasn't sure if I could pull it off, but I thought I would give it a try. I thought about all the questions they could possibly ask me in an interview, like "Why do you want to be a destination representative? Why do you think you would be a good representative? What does good customer service mean to you?" I wrote 10 questions down and then wrote out my answers to all of them. I then called a good friend of mine who was fluent in Spanish and asked for a big favor. I asked her if she could translate all the questions and answers for me into Spanish.

She did. She helped me with the pronunciation, and I memorized each of the answers.

I remember arriving at the interview and feeling nervous and nauseous. The interview started off easy enough, and it was going really well; I could feel it. Then, it was time for the dreaded test. My heart was beating out of my chest. The interviewer said, "So now I am going to test your Spanish, okay?"

"Okay," I replied with a smile. *NO! Not okay!* is what I was thinking.

"So tell me, Sonia, why do you want to be a destination representative?" he asked in Spanish. I almost fell off my chair. I know this one! I answered with my memorized answer.

Next question. "Why do you think you would be a good representative?" I know this one too! I answered with my memorized answer. I couldn't believe it. He asked me four questions, and I had the answers to all of them! Three months later, I was working in Varadero, Cuba, as a destination representative.

Mind you, I had to spend those three months between getting the job and actually beginning work learning a new language, and believe me, it wasn't easy. But it was something I wanted so much that I was willing to work hard to get it.

What is amazing is that I spent the next four years working as a destination representative for various companies, and I lived in Cuba, Colombia, and Mexico. Those four years were some of the most memorable and incredible years of my life. I could easily have been stopped by the obstacle that was presented in front of me—not knowing how to speak Spanish—but instead I chose to think outside the box, step outside the box, and ultimately live outside the box.

During those four years, I became very present to the way people are stopped by these types of obstacles all the time. It really fascinated me. Foreign travelers would always come up to me and say, "Wow, I wish I could do the job that you are doing. I would absolutely love living in paradise and spending my winters here."

My response would always be the same: "Then do it! If I can do it, so can you!"

This is the answer I would always hear from people: "Oh, no, I really wish I could, but I can't. I don't speak Spanish."

Challenge the Status Quo

Don't let obstacles stop you from living your greatest life. There will be obstacles, no question, but you can overcome them. You may have to work hard, but it is possible. Simply think outside the box and be different. Don't follow the crowd.

It takes a lot of courage to live life on your own terms. You will be faced with a lot of fear. *What if I fail? What if people laugh at me? What if I make a fool of myself? What if I am making a mistake?* Those are all normal fearful questions that come up when taking the road less traveled, the road to your greatest life.

The answer to all of them? So what. Do it anyway.

The next time you begin to feel fear, simply remind yourself that fear is just another emotion and that all emotions are generated through your thoughts. Your thoughts are causing you to feel fearful.

So what if you fail? So what if people laugh at you? So what if you make a fool of yourself? So what if you make a mistake? *So what?* It doesn't mean anything anyway—except what you choose to make it mean. If you make a mistake, pick yourself up, dust yourself off, learn what you are supposed to learn, and continue moving forward. You may be required to shift your direction a bit, but you must move forward.

Now ask yourself these questions: *What if I succeed? What if it all works out beautifully? What if it works out better than I could ever imagine?* How does that feel? I'm sure it feels great. But what really matters is the journey. What matters is that you are living your life true to yourself. You may or may not reach the destination you desire. You may in fact reach an even better destination—better than you ever thought possible.

Be flexible. Be courageous. Be a maverick.

It is all unfolding the way it should.

Conclusion: Rising From the Ashes

Mastering the 20 lessons in this book will have a profound impact on your life. As you maneuver your way through the tough times, imagine yourself as a phoenix rising from the ashes. With every end there is a new beginning.

A new beginning is in front of you now.

Wherever you are on your journey right now, always remember these very important words: *Don't give up.* Never, ever give up. When you are just about to give up is when things are about to turn around.

Life can seem very dark at times, but just hang in there; the light *will* begin to shine again. You may not know how it will happen exactly, but simply trust. Just because you can't figure out exactly how to get out of your situation right now, it doesn't mean things won't turn around.

When you are stuck and feeling helpless, confused, and just want to give up, take a time-out. Surrender to the moment. Let go of trying to figure things out and just simply trust and have faith that everything will happen the way it is supposed to. Set an intention that everything will work out, and then let it go and move forward.

Miracles DO Happen

Around the same time I was going through my difficult situation, I visited a good friend of mine who was experiencing some serious financial problems. She was unable to pay her rent and would be evicted from her apartment if she didn't come up with the money in the next week. It was a very stressful time for her. She tried to figure out how to get herself out of this bad situation. She attempted several different things to quickly generate cash, but for some reason, nothing worked. Unfortunately, I wasn't in any financial position at the time to help her myself.

"If I could just figure out a way to manifest $2,000, everything would be fine. Just $2,000 that's it, that's all I have to come up with," she said.

"You can do that," I said. "You still have a few days to pull it off! Actually, instead of setting the intention of manifesting $2,000, why don't you set the intention of manifesting $5,000! That will keep you going for next month too!"

I was trying to be a good, supportive friend, but honestly, I had no idea how such a thing would be possible. We were throwing those statements out but we had no real plan behind how the money was going to appear in the next few days. It all sounded very Pollyanna-ish.

She finally decided to surrender, and said, "I am surrendering to everything that is happening. I am allowing what is supposed to happen to happen. If I am supposed to leave this place, I will. If I am supposed to stay here, something will happen to make it happen. It will all work out. I surrender to it all."

"Sounds good to me. Just let it go for now." I said. "Hey, I have plans to meet my friend Jenn for lunch shortly, you should come too."

"Sure," she responded.

A few minutes later, we put on our jackets and hopped in the car. The 20-minute ride to the restaurant was filled with laughter and fun small-talk. We were simply enjoying the present, living in the moment, and loving life.

I was excited to meet with Jenn because I hadn't seen her for several months and there was so much catching up to do. We all had a beautiful time having lunch, chatting, laughing, and sharing stories. After about two hours, it was time to say our goodbyes, and Jenn said to my friend, "Let's keep in touch. Give me your number and I will call you."

My friend replied, "Well, actually, I'm probably going to have a different number very shortly because I'm moving. So I will call you instead."

"You're moving? Well, that's exciting! Where are you moving to?" Jenn asked, a bit surprised considering that this major event wasn't mentioned at all throughout lunch.

"Actually, I don't know where I'm moving to yet."

"I don't understand," Jenn said, completely confused.

"I'm being evicted."

"What?!? What do you mean?" she asked in shock.

"I'm being evicted. I didn't really want to talk about it during lunch." She said. "I'm having some financial problems right now, and I haven't been able to come up with the rent so I'm being evicted. But don't worry, everything will work itself out."

"Evicted? Are you kidding me? How much money do you need? I'll lend you the money," Jenn said.

"Oh, no. I can't accept money from you. It wouldn't feel right. Plus, I don't know when I'd be able to pay you back. Thank you so much for offering to help though. That means a lot to me. I'll be fine. Don't worry."

"I insist." Jenn said. "How much do you need?"

"No. No. I can't accept money from you."

Jenn then went into her purse and pulled out a checkbook and a pen.

"Okay then, if you won't tell me how much you need, I'll write you a check for the amount that feels right to me."

I was stunned at was happening. Jenn had only met my friend once before, they barely knew each other. Was Jenn really going to lend her money? I couldn't believe it. She began writing the check. She tore it off from the checkbook and handed it to my friend, saying, "Here you go. This should help you pay your rent and keep you going for a little while. You can pay me back when you are 75 years old."

My friend took the check, looked at it, and tears began to well up in her eyes.

"Thank you. I don't know what to say."

"You're welcome. Someone helped me out several years ago when I was down and out. I am just paying it forward," Jenn said with a big smile on her face.

The check was for $7,500.

This is a perfect example of how things can turn around in a split second. Often things change in ways that you couldn't even imagine. You hear stories of miracles like these happening all the time, often even more dramatic and unbelievable. If it has happened to others, it can happen to you.

This isn't to say you should just sit down, not do anything, and wait for something incredible to land in your lap. What I *am* saying is, have faith that something incredible will be sent your way. Do what you need to do, but surrender the control of how it is "supposed" to happen.

Just know that miracles do happen. Sometimes they don't look like miracles at first, but in due time, their brilliance and beauty will shine.

Epílogue:
And So It Is

When I think back to all that happened in my life, it almost doesn't feel real; it feels like it was a dream. That's what happens with time. The memories do not have any hold on me, but are there to remind me where I've been, what I've learned, how I've grown—and where I'm headed. I am now able to look back and focus on all the great times, of which there were many, even in the midst of all the chaos.

I know that I will experience other challenges as time moves forward. That's life. It's all part of the journey. It's not good, it's not bad, it just *is*. I am okay with that.

I am in awe of the way everything unfolds the way it is supposed to. Today, I am so grateful for all that has happened. I am grateful for the man I once called my soulmate, and that he came into my life when he did. Although today our lives have taken different paths, we still maintain a beautiful friendship filled with mutual respect and love in our hearts that will last forever. I am grateful for him helping me grow and blossom into something I never even dreamed was possible.

I am grateful for experiencing what it feels like to be in financial distress, because it makes today's financial abundance that much sweeter.

I am grateful for all the amazing and loving people in my life who were there when I needed them the most, and who picked me up when I was knocked down.

I am grateful for the health issues I have experienced. They were a reminder of how precious life is and how quickly it can be taken from us.

Now, I am so much better equipped. The lessons I've learned, I will keep with me forever. They will be my saving grace the next time I get knocked down. Life is great today, and it will continue to be from this day forward. How do I know that? Because that is what I choose. The events that happen today and in the future no longer have a hold on me.

What happens doesn't matter because I hold the key to my own peace and my own happiness.

...and so do you.

Resources

Unsinkable Online Community and Free Resources

If you wish to continue the conversation on how to be unsinkable and move forward in life, please visit the Be Unsinkable Website at *www.beunsinkable.com*. There you will find a supportive community where you can share your stories and comments, and communicate with others on the same journey. You will also find an abundance of free resources such as videos, articles, and audio recordings that take this subject to an even deeper level.

Programs, Workshops, Teleseminars, and More!

If you wish to experience Sonia live, either via the Internet or in person, please visit her personal Website at *www.leadoutloud.com.* There you will find information on the many programs, live teleseminars, workshops, and products she offers.

Project Unsinkable

Contribution to others and making a difference is very important to Sonia. In fact, she has participated in many humanitarian trips around the world in the last few years, which has had a profound impact on her life.

If you wish to help make a difference in someone's life and want to contribute your time or money to a special cause, please visit the Project Unsinkable Website at *www.projectunsinkable.com.* There, you will find the most recent humanitarian initiatives Sonia and her team are working on.

Appendix: Biographies of Unsinkable Contributors

Melinda Asztalos

www.lifepositivebydesign.com

Melinda Asztalos is a parent coach, a speaker, and the founder of Life Positive by Design. With more than two decades of spiritual study and a deep understanding of human psychology, Melinda assists and supports parents in accessing their own inner wisdom as they explore the benefits of conscious parenting.

Janet Bray Attwood

www.thepassiontest.com

Janet Attwood is a world-renowned speaker and *New York Times* best-selling author who has taught The Passion Test to hundreds of thousands of people in the United States, Canada, Europe, and India. Janet has presented alongside the Dalai Lama, Sir Richard Branson, Byron

Katie, and others. She has personally trained more than 500 Passion Test Facilitators around the world. In following her passions, Janet has interviewed more than 100 Masters from around the world.

Joann Brnjas

Joann learned firsthand what it's like to parent a young adult battling a merciless sarcoma. Still learning to live with the grief over the departure of her much-loved Samantha from this world, Joann shares the way her daughter's body succumbed to the disease but their hope did not. Joann lives in Ontario, Canada, with her husband, Joe, and cat, Minxie, and spends as much time as possible with her other children, grandchildren, parents, and friends. When she is not working in the financial/insurance business sector, she is attending theology classes, which will one day complement her MBA.

Sam Cawthorn

www.samcawthorn.com

Sam is a thought leader and CEO for Empowering Enterprises and has been featured in USA Today and The New York Times. He is the 2009 Young Australian of the Year for Tasmania. In October 2006, he was involved in a car accident in which he died. He was resusicated, but left with major injuries. He is now a hugely successful keynote speaker.

Cynthia Kersey

www.unstoppablefoundation.org

Cynthia Kersey is the best-selling author of two books, *Unstoppable* and *Unstoppable Women*. She is a speaker, entrepreneur, team coach, and Chief Humanitarian Officer of her nonprofit foundation whose focus is to ensure that every child on the planet has access to the life-long gift of education. In her powerful program, Unstoppable Giving, Cynthia not only inspires individuals to give but also provides entrepreneurs with a practical action plan for increasing their bottom line, expanding their business, creating customer evangelists, and becoming invigorated by their life and business by integrating generosity as a business philosophy. Cynthia embodies her message and has integrated giving and contribution into her life and business for more than a decade.

Gina Mollicone-Long

www.ginaml.com

Gina Mollicone-Long is an international best-selling author, compelling speaker, and serial entrepreneur with a mission to reveal greatness in individuals, teams, and organizations. She is the cofounder of two multinational corporate team-building and training companies, and she has a breadth of corporate experience that ranges from giants such as Procter & Gamble to high-tech incubators, small start-ups, and even nonprofits. An avid world traveler, Gina's experiences with diverse cultural perspectives gives her programs universal relevance that helps her connect with audiences everywhere. Since 1998, she has trained, coached, or spoken to tens of thousands of people globally, including sharing the stage with Bob Proctor from the blockbuster movie, *The Secret.*

Bob Proctor

www.bobproctor.com

Bob Proctor is widely regarded as one of the living masters and teachers of the Law of Attraction, and has worked in the area of mind potential for more than 40 years. He is the best-selling author of *You Were Born Rich*, and has transformed the lives of millions through his books, seminars, courses, and personal coaching. His work descends directly from the father of success philosophy, Andrew Carnegie, the great financier and philanthropist. Carnegie's secrets inspired and enthused Napoleon Hill, whose book *Think and Grow Rich* in turn inspired a whole genre of success philosophy books; Napoleon Hill, in turn, passed the baton on to Earl Nightingale, who has since placed it in Bob Proctor's capable hands. His company, LifeSuccess Productions, is headquartered in Phoenix, Arizona, and operates globally.

Marci Shimoff

www.happyfornoreason.com

Marci Shimoff is a #1 *New York Times* best-selling author, a world-renowned transformational teacher, and an expert on happiness, success, and unconditional love. Her books include the *New York Times* best-sellers *Love for No Reason* and *Happy for No Reason,* and six titles in the phenomenally successful Chicken Soup for the Woman's Soul series. Her books have sold more than 14 million copies worldwide in 33 languages. Marci is also a featured teacher in the international film and book sensation, *The Secret.*

Index

A

Al-Anon, 55
Alcoholics Anonymous, 33
anger, 39, 42, 46, 51, 91, 94, 131, 135-136, 141
Attwood, Janet Bray, 81-88, 181-182
Asztalos, Melinda, 70

B

beliefs,
    empowering, 102, 104-105
    limiting, 101-105, 125
breathing, deep, 119-120
Brnjas, Joann, 146, 182
Buddha, 80

C

Cawthorn, Sam, 75-79, 182
change, 61, 73, 97, 99, 101, 165
change, saying yes to, 41-42

childhood, 102,
choice, 38-39, 41-42, 62, 65, 67, 70, 72, 93, 96-99
circle of light, 53-56, 122
clarity, 50, 62, 116-120, 125
closed door, 106-109, 113, 161-162
compassion, 53, 143
crying, 27, 48-49, 51

D

deep breathing, 119-120
denial, 34, 65, 76, 149
door,
    closed, 106-109, 113, 161-162
    open, 106, 109, 113, 161-162

E

empowering beliefs, 102, 104-105

energy, negative, 50, 116, 121-122

environment, positive, 121, 123

exercise, 116, 130, 134, 136-137

F

failure, 97-99

fear, 42, 67-68, 73-74, 142-143, 150, 168

feedback, 97,99

feelings, negative, 49-50, 91-92, 131, 136

finances, 103-104

forgiveness, 132-134, 137, 141-142, 146

G

giving, 153-158

God, 47, 80, 85, 136, 148, 150, 160

gratitude, 67-68, 70, 100, 142, 144, 146, 155

group therapy, 52

guidance, 46, 55, 68-69, 73

H

Happy for No Reason, 139, 185

hope, 29, 33, 72, 80, 87-88, 135, 146, 149-150, 156

I

inner wisdom, 67

interpretation, 92-94, 100, 102, 138

intuition, 82, 124-125

J

journaling, 51, 64, 119

journey, 49, 57, 62, 68-70, 72, 116, 127, 147, 150, 169, 177, 179
awakened, 72-74
in-between, 73
life is a, 38
safe, 72
your, 42, 171

L

laughter, 119

Law of Attraction, 29-30, 50, 184

Law of Attraction Plain and Simple, The, 29, 71, 112

Law of Giving and
    Receiving, 154-155, 158
Lead Out Loud, 29, 107
limiting beliefs, 101-105, 125
Live Life Out Loud Miracle
    Weekend, 133
Love for No Reason, 139-
    140, 185

M

*Mastering the Law of
    Attraction*, 107, 110
meditation, 82, 117, 143
Mollicone-Long, Gina,
    94-100, 183-184
money, 101-102, 154,157, 180

N

nature, 118, 130
nutrition, 120-121

O

open door, 106, 109, 113,
    161-162
opportunity,58, 67, 69,
    78-79, 106, 133, 144,
    161-162

P

pain, 25-28, 49-51, 62-63, 68,
    70, 72, 92, 106, 129, 131,
    156-158
past, the, 71-73, 126-127,
    130, 133
    holding onto the, 25, 71
peace, 50, 67, 72, 84, 125,
    136, 138, 143, 178
    finding, 38-40
    inner, 116, 133
    sense of, 36, 130
perception, 92, 136, 138
positive environment, 121, 123
process of living, 99
Proctor, Bob, 43-48, 184

R

receiving, 142, 154-155
recovery, 42
recycling, 57
red flag, 30, 32, 124
relationships, 26, 33, 57-58,
    67, 71, 74, 101, 103-104,
    116, 129, 151
resentment, 39, 46, 59, 131,
    135, 141

S

Samantha, 133-136, 146-151

Secret, The, 29, 43, 109, 184-185

self-compassion, 141

self-inquiry, 57-58, 100

self-reflection, 58

self-talk, 103-104

shield of light, 122

Shimoff, Marci, 139, 184

silver lining, 72, 133-134, 136-137, 146

soulmate, 26, 31, 57, 101

suffering, 39, 61, 70, 92, 101,

surrendering, 62-63, 69, 127

T

Tapping the Source, 74

Think or Sink, 94

thoughts,
  bad, 45-46
  good, 45
  negative, 46, 70
  shifting, 92, 94, 106, 109, 113, 137
  your, 71, 92-93, 100, 106, 109, 113-114, 119, 132-133, 136-137, 168

time out, taking a, 117-118

U

unconditional love, 38, 53, 138-140, 142-144, 184

universe, 67, 80-81, 88, 98, 140, 160

W

wisdom, inner, 67

About the Author

Sonia Ricotti is a leading expert in personal and professional transformation. She travels around the world as a top-rated professional speaker, inspiring people everywhere to live their greatest lives, and has shared the stage with some of the biggest transformational experts of our time. She is also the #1 best-selling author of *The Law of Attraction Plain and Simple: Create the Extraordinary Life That You Deserve*.

She is the president of Lead Out Loud, a company that offers inspirational products, videos, and workshops that transform people's lives. She is also the creator and host of the popular Be Unsinkable Teleseminar Series, in which she interviews some of the biggest transformational leaders from around the globe. Sonia has also become a YouTube sensation with her inspirational videos, viewed by more than 3 million people around the world.

Sonia believes in giving back to the world and has participated in and led several humanitarian trips around the globe.

To find out more about Sonia's keynote presentations, workshops, books, videos, and personal appearances, you can contact her at:

Lead Out Loud, Inc.

193 Church St., P.O. Box 1221

Oakville, Ontario

L6J 5C7 Canada

Phone: (416) 804-1974

E-mail: info@leadoutloud.com

www.leadoutloud.com